the
FIRST
GENERATION

Bridging the Generational Gap of Mental Health

EILEEN STREMMING

New Degree Press

ISBN   978-1-64137-320-3 *Paperback*

          978-1-64137-620-4 *Ebook*

Life is worth living when we give it meaning.

To my sisters Erika and Eliza,
I truly do not think I would be here without you
both, being your sister brings meaning to my
life. This book is dedicated to you both.

To my non-blood related best friends, without your words
of love and reassurance, I would never feel strong enough
to keep moving forward. I will be eternally grateful
for your friendship and reminders that my life is worth
living when my brain tries to tell me otherwise.

And to my fellow humans that are [not so]
secretly fighting their own battles with their
brains, we are stronger than our thoughts.

CONTENTS

"I want future generations to know that we are a
people who see our differences as a great gift, that
we're a people who value the dignity and worth
of every citizen—man and woman, young and old,
black and white, Latino and Asian, immigrant and
Native American, gay and straight, Americans
with mental illness or physical disability."

—PRESIDENT BARACK OBAMA

Dear Reader

This book will help us to normalize conversations regarding mental health. I think that this will allow us to truly start conversations and help us to break the stigma. I think that there are four steps in order to help us normalize mental health. These suggestions are just general guidelines that I have found useful, and they should not be taken as professional or medical advice. By no means am I a licensed professional, so I do suggest that you should seek professional help if there is something bothering you.

Feel free to jump around the chapters; this book is separated into sections depending on the theme.

Do treat each chapter independently, and do not feel the need to read this book in order. However you decide to read this book, there are important points to understand from each chapter. While they are connected, you can read this how you please.

I hope that you know that you can make a change.

I hope that no matter how alone you might feel because of your experiences, you know that there is someone else who has gone through something similar.

Realizing that we all have our own struggles—and that our peers and family members have their own as well—will hopefully result in a mutual understanding and healthier relationships that do not require the avoidance of certain conversations or topics.

We all have power in teaching ourselves how to be better, how to understand better, and how to be more empathetic about things we may not understand.

This book will leave you empowered in your ability to realize that you have strength in your voice. Talk about what you go through. Grow through what you go through.

It is up to you and me to talk about what we have been through. No more hiding our experiences. No more feeling guilty for our valid feelings. We are all going through something, and you should know that you are never alone.

If we can talk about our mental health normally, I truly believe *that* will normalize it. If we are embarrassed to discuss our everyday realities, then we are doing an injustice to ourselves.

We need to do our part: we need to acknowledge our experiences, hold ourselves accountable, discuss our experiences, be better and do better.

We can do this, and we can do it together.

Introduction

Mental health is not a journey that sails smoothly whenever we want it to—much like the ocean, it has its waves and can be a bit unpredictable. Sometimes the waters are too rough and quite difficult to navigate, especially alone. Sometimes, it has its moments of calm, and everything seems like it is going to be okay.

After finishing my senior year of high school, I thought that a change of scenery and being on my own would be good for me. At the time, I did not realize how empowering independence actually is. It can also be liberating for those that have been in situations that are less than optimal—allowing for a lot of growth and new opportunities to truly think for oneself.

However, independence is also a double-edged sword. I did not give myself a summer to say good-bye to my friends because I started university in a new city, without any of my friends, just three weeks after graduation. It is not always best to jump into an independent lifestyle if you are not quite ready for it. It can be difficult to transition and more harmful than positive. This sudden change, without the proper tools, can be detrimental to your mental health.

Before I even made the decision to start school in the summer, my mother said to me, "It is your future, I do not want you to go to college and then feel alone and hopeless."

I thought my depression was purely situational, that being my own person and living by myself would be good for me. For a while, I was simply enjoying life, and everything was calm. Everything was okay.

Come autumn, I fell right back into my old thinking pattern. I was sad again, and all I wanted to do was sleep. I got back on my medication.

My mother wanted me to stay in Jacksonville and attend the University of North Florida to live with my sister. She said, "You will have your freedom but when you break down at night, you will have your *Ate*." I began to regret that I had left home and tried to do this by myself.

I lived in an apartment off-campus, without a car. My friends lived on campus—so it was hard for me to get out of my room when I was already in a mood. Sure, I had friends, but many of them had their own things going on, so I often felt burdensome.

If you have ever felt like a burden, if you have ever felt like you were alone in your journey, that is a reason why you are reading this book. If you have ever wanted to talk about mental health but have been afraid to because of reactions from your family...that is why you are reading this book.

In the United States alone, one in five adults has a mental health condition. The ADAA has noted that "Almost 75% of people with mental disorders remain untreated in developing countries." And Mental Health America notes that 56% of American adults with a mental illness do not receive treatment.

Understanding mental health is still relatively new because there are so many factors that go into mental illness.

Is it environmental?

Is it situational?

Is it a chemical imbalance?

For far too long, mental health has been pushed aside and misunderstood. Psychology is a relatively new science compared to physics or astronomy—which have been around since the 4th Century BCE—and our understanding of mental health is still subjective.

Unfortunately in 2019, mental health is still being stigmatized, and this should not be this case. What is stigma? While the definition of stigma can vary slightly—the basis of a stigma is having a distinctive characteristic that allows one to be made "different." Oftentimes, it can cause us to be ostracized because we are not the "norm." According to Peter Byrne, former Director of Public Education for Royal College of Psychiatry, "Stigma is defined as a sign of disgrace or discredit, which sets a person apart from others." Mayo Clinic defines it as, "when someone views you in a negative way because you have a distinguishing characteristic or personal trait that is thought to be, or actually is, a disadvantage (a negative stereotype)."

There are a few problems when it comes to mental health. People are often unaware or uneducated—or even worse; they have these preconceptions that allow them to continue thinking that people with mental health issues have "decided" that they are unwell or are doing something wrong.

In 2017, in California, a survey aptly named the California Well-Being Survey was used to determine the stigma encompassing mental illness and discrimination.

Researchers Wong, Collins, Cerully, Seelam, and Roth's key findings include:

- Most adults in California with mental health problems believe that those with a mental illness face more prejudice and discrimination.
- Asian Americans report levels of higher self-stigma (in terms of feeling inferior to those without a mental health condition) as well as believe—less than white people—that those with mental health problems are not contributing members of society.
- Latinos interviewed in English report higher levels of self-stigma (in terms of feeling embarrassed, ashamed, and not understood), as well as reported, less than whites, that they would conceal any potential problem.

- Latinos interviewed in Spanish were the least likely to use any mental health services although they reported lower levels of stigma in comparison to whites.

When I moved, I thought that I was good mentally and that I would not fall into any sadness and would not allow darkness to overcome me. I "finished" therapy and I did not think it was necessary for me to find someone close to school. My close friends urged me to find someone again and even promised that they would come with me to my appointments.

"You are not alone, Eileen. You are never alone. You have got me," they would remind me.

Granted, there were some people around me that did not take me seriously, and just wrote off my feelings like I was being too dramatic. But there will always be people who do not believe in you—there are always people that think your life *seems* too good for anything to be wrong.

I tried to find another therapist that fall but I became frustrated when she thought my problem was simply not eating right or not taking the right vitamins. So I gave up. It took me another year and a half to find a therapist that helps me deal with everything when I feel like I just *cannot* do anything.

I asked him to *please* not enable me or make me feel like I get into depressed moods because I'm "eating poorly." I remember one of the first things that happened after telling him about my previous experiences in therapy. He said to me, "I do reality-based therapy, so I will not bullsh*t you." And thank goodness, he helps me to ground myself, hold myself accountable and be better.

We should be opening up the conversation and making it acceptable to discuss our emotions and mental illnesses. We should not make people feel like they are abnormal when their heads are unwell.

We would not hassle someone with an obvious physical disability by telling them they "just need to get out and get some fresh air"—we would not even judge someone with a broken leg or pester them to do things that they are obviously unable to do. So why do we completely disregard our peers, friends, and family with mental illnesses?

It is simply not fair. We need to take a step back, recognize signs, learn, understand and realize that mental illness is not that absurd.

A mental illness warrants attention. We cannot help but notice someone on crutches, but when's the last time you were able to identify someone with depression or with anxious thoughts? These illnesses are not seen, so we might often think, "It's only in your head!" That, by definition, is not wrong, although it is slightly insensitive. It is a mental illness for a reason; it is just that—mental. It is so hard to identify sometimes because some people are extremely good at hiding their illness. If we can learn how to recognize it before it is too late, then we are on the right path.

Everyone's journey with mental health is continuous and part of that ongoing process is to educate others along the way. Hopefully, by being an advocate for mental health normalization, other people will feel more empowered and realize that it is not such a scary thing to talk about. It is scary to be the first person to do something, but it can also be extremely rewarding.

While it is difficult to live with, it can be equally as hard for those around us to understand it. So, any progress forward is a step in the right direction. Being able to speak about mental health freely is one way we are able to normalize it.

While it is hard to talk to family members whose experiences growing up were very different from ours, it does not mean we cannot break down barriers and find common ground to discuss something that is not spoken about, but is so incredibly important that it deserves a conversation. We need to find a support system that allows us to have these conversations.

- In my own experience, I have found that my mom's initial push normalized treatment and my passion for breaking the stigma.
- Jady, with all the ups and downs, found that while her parents are still learning, her biggest support system is found in her siblings.
- Jane found on her journey that sometimes it's best to do what we need to for us to get better, instead of worrying about what the people around us may think.
- Nicole learned that it is okay to get help and it is okay to take medication too.

On our journeys, sometimes we might discover that our biggest advocates are our parents—although we may have refused to talk about our mental health with them simply because we were afraid they would not understand.

Sometimes, the best confidants that we get are the ones we are born with—our siblings.

Sometimes it just takes one other person speaking out about their experiences with mental illness for us to say, "Hey, me too."

Over the past three years, I have learned so much about psychology in general and myself, and have become more vocal about mental health. I believe the steps to normalizing mental health are to:

1. **Acknowledge.** We need to acknowledge the differences that might make it difficult for some to discuss their mental health problems—especially in immigrant families.
2. **Be accountable.** We need to hold ourselves accountable and learn how to recognize the signs of mental illness.
3. **Talk.** We need to learn how to talk about it—because it can be very hard—with friends, with mental health professionals, and with our loved ones.
4. **Improve.** And after we are comfortable talking about it, then we can start to do something about it: getting help and doing better for ourselves and for anyone else on their own mental health journey.

These four stages and steps form the basis of this book and a path for each of us to change the stigma.

We need to normalize the discussion regarding mental health and that is my hope for this book. I hope that this book will start conversations in attempts to normalize talks about mental health problems. And after we do these four things, then we can really begin to de-stigmatize mental health.

I will be sharing my experiences as a child of a first-generation immigrant as well as that of my sister. I am also including several stories from other children of immigrants, as well as some experiences with mental health from those that are not children of immigrants. Additionally, I will include insights from experts in the field.

Our struggles are struggles and it is important to talk about them.

So, let us talk about it.

Part I:
ACKNOWLEDGE

Chapter 1:
A Push in the Right Direction

"Where are you from?"

"Oh, I was born and raised here in Jacksonville, Florida."

"No, but like, where are you *really* from?"

"I—I'm from Mandarin? It's like South Jax?"

"Okay—I'm sorry. What ethnicity are you?"

"Oh, I see, I'm Filipino."

I would often chalk up these conversations to inappropriate curiosity. But there's more to it.

As people, we want to categorize everything and everyone—whether they are a certain race or ethnicity, whether they are male or female. We feel it is important for us to inform ourselves based on what categories we place people in.

Research has found that our heuristics—also called rules of thumb or mental shortcuts—allow us to go into more positive social interactions if we know what someone's background is.

I have had many conversations with people that had *just* met me and were wondering what ethnicity I was. A few years back, I no longer wanted my ethnic background to define me and I decided I would have fun with people that were so fixated on finding out what my ethnic background was.

As the child of two immigrants, my culture has always been a huge part of my identity. While some children do not desire to draw attention to identify with ethnic background, I always mentioned that I was Filipino. In elementary school, it was always one of my introduction points—despite the fact that my name does not sound at all "exotic."

Moreover, growing up Filipino in Florida in the 2000s meant that I would not completely be the same as my all-American classmates. I loved the fact that I was unique until I started getting made fun of for being "chinky." The first time I realized that it was something I could be ostracized for, I was in shock. I did not think my fun fact would turn into something that people would make fun of me for. Kids can be pretty mean once they decide that your differences are not a good thing.

I remember a kid in elementary school saying loud enough for me to hear, "Haha! Eileen has slanty eyes! She's Asian!"

After this interaction and being made aware of this growing up, I often felt like I was less beautiful than my white friends because the standard of beauty in the United States was not someone who looked like me. Instead, the ideal girl that I believed all of the boys liked had fairer skin than me and lighter hair than me—and her eyes? Oh, beautiful colors—blue, green, or hazel. No one would find my dark brown eyes beautiful.

The majority of my peers are white, and many of my girl-friends are white. So, I will admit it, sometimes my race was something that was not always at the forefront of my mind—I have also been told that I act "really white for an Asian." So, people would often question, "What are you, *really?*" after I told them I am Filipino.

A good rule of thumb: if it makes you uncomfortable to ask, then maybe you should not—no matter how much you want to know. Asking what someone's ethnicity is to break the ice is a terrible idea. And do not even get me started on the dreaded "*What* are you?" ...*what* am I? I am a strong and intelligent young woman, that is *what* I am.

Social psychologists have mentioned that by asking, "What are you?" it mostly communicates that you are more curious about someone's background than interested in being respect-ful. Instead of being so focused on what someone "is" and ask-ing "what" they are, ask different questions about him or her.

While this was just a small problem I realized I would have to overcome, my sisters and I would have so many conversations just like this over the years regarding our race. This would make our experience growing up slightly different from my friends with non-immigrant parents.

I have two beautiful and strong sisters, one older and one younger. I absolutely adore my sisters, love them more than anyone in the world, and I would not want to change a thing. I have my parents to thank for giving me my first two best friends and letting us become each others' confidants.

My parents came to the United States in their teenage years and attended high school together in Key West, Florida. My mother always told us that we needed to work hard in school; she was never a "Tiger Mom" per se, but how successful we were in school was incredibly important to both her and my father. They came to the United States and gave us the best fighting chance they could, so they really want the best for us. For us to do well in school means that their coming to the U.S. was not a waste.

Growing up as a first-generation child meant trying to reach the high expectations set by my parents and myself—every single day education seemed to reign supreme. Getting A's was the expectation, getting B's was acceptable, and getting a C was just plain old disappointing. We were applauded for good work, but not necessarily rewarded for it simply because it was expected of us. My classmates would say they got the newest toys like a Razor scooter for their last report card while we simply got a "good job" for straight A's and maybe a nice dinner. It was quite difficult for me to not be competitive about good grades with my sisters. I always sought validation via my good grades and I still do.

Growing up, I became known as "The Smart One" among my sisters to family and friends. I used to be jealous of my sisters—I always felt as if I had to work harder, especially in school, for attention from one of my parents. I strived to win awards, participate in extracurriculars, be on a club committee, or be accepted to honor societies just for some validation. Somewhere in there, I started doing it a little for my own satisfaction, but I felt like the typical middle child—the overachiever—doing more than what my parents asked for. All they asked us to do was work hard and do well in school, but I felt like I had to do more.

Complaining about anything was difficult because we were incredibly fortunate to only really have to worry about our education. If we ever tried to complain, my mom would remind us,

"I came to the United States at 11 years old. Lola and Lolo told me that if I wanted anything, I would have to work for it and buy it myself. So that's what I did, I got a job as a cashier at 15. I never asked for anything from them. I bought my first car and I bought all of my clothes by myself."

For anyone that young, that was something to be proud of. And considering that my mother had only been in the United States for four years at that point, she had done an amazing job of assimilating. But this does not mean money was easy to come by. Money was a burden for my parents, and is still an ongoing problem for us—so doing our best educationally was all that my parents asked of us. They never wanted us to worry about finances like they had to.

While I did not have to worry so much about money until college, I definitely had different worries. And while it may seem typical for a teenage girl to worry if people liked her, I was constantly wondering if people were secretly making fun of me behind my back, or if I had said something that might have given them reason to make fun of me. I was paranoid that my friends were not really my friends and that they were saying mean things when I was not around. Additionally, I hated public speaking and I hated the feeling in my stomach I would get before I would have to present anything in front of an audience.

Talking about these things with our family members is somewhat difficult. Anything that seemingly comes close to confrontation is a pretty hard feat in itself. If possible, my family would rather text than have conversations in person. But in the seventh grade, my parents gave us the hardest news I would ever have to hear in the 12 years of my young life.

One evening in the fall of 2010, my parents took my sisters and me to dinner. "You guys can order anything and everything you want." My sisters and I exchanged a look that conveyed, "Hmm, something is off." However, we remained happily ignorant to the news my parents were waiting to share, and we ate our burgers and drank our milkshakes. We paid the check, then headed out to drop my mom off at the hospital where she worked. Silence. Then suddenly,

"We have some news," my father began, "we want you to know that we will always be a family. And your Mama and I will always love you guys. This has nothing to do with you."

I started crying because I had a bad feeling in my stomach, it felt like my stomach was being twisted and turned in ways it should not. It felt as if butterflies of excitement were dying in my stomach instead of fluttering.

"Nothing is going to change. We're just separating. We'll still do things as a family."

Much to my displeasure, this was untrue. We never did things as a family again after my dad moved out the following spring. This was the first time in my life I felt sadness. I cannot attribute my feelings of sadness to depression because both of my sisters were sad too. *This was normal,* I thought. I did not feel sadness that profoundly until I was a senior in high school.

Fast forward five years. In the fall of 2015, I started to apply for colleges while juggling my first job, my first boyfriend, my role as a club president, and a general uneasiness and anxiety about my future. I had been feeling anxious for a while but I started having random crying spells. I did not want to do anything because I had no motivation. There was always plenty that needed to be done, but I would come home from school exhausted just from thinking about it. And I was sleeping a lot and not eating much of anything.

Moreover, I had fainted for the first time in public, so a few days later, I went to my doctor to ask if something was wrong with me. He said to me, "I am going to prescribe you Zoloft. A lot of high school seniors feel this kind of stress and it will help you feel 'normal' and less anxious."

This was the man who had taken care of me for 17 years of my life, even after we had made a move to the other side of town, 30 minutes away. I literally trusted this man with my life. After talking to me for a little while and determining that I was stressed because of college applications, he prescribed me an SSRI (Selective Serotonin Reuptake Inhibitor). I did not realize at the time that doctors prescribe SSRIs to people with depression and anxiety.

SSRIs, according to Mayo Clinic, "are the most commonly prescribed antidepressants. They can ease symptoms of moderate to severe depression, are relatively safe and typically cause fewer side effects than other types of antidepressants do."

SSRIs work by increasing levels of serotonin in the brain. Serotonin is the neurotransmitter that is thought to be responsible for regulating happiness, mood, and anxiety. According to Mayo Clinic, "SSRIs block the reabsorption, or reuptake of serotonin in the brain—making more serotonin available. SSRIs are referred to as selective because they seem to primarily affect serotonin and not other neurotransmitters." Additionally, studies have shown that there is a link between depression and low levels of serotonin—which has also been shown to affect our sleep and bowel movements. The symptoms of depression include not only loss of interest in things that you used to enjoy, but also a change in appetite and insomnia (sleeping too little) or hypersomnia (sleeping too much).

My pediatrician also recommended that I get some blood tests to see if there was a reason for my exhaustion and my fainting. They noticed an irregularity in my blood— they assumed anemia (several years later, they still have not confirmed if it is anemia, but there is still an irregularity).

However, I started taking iron supplements and Zoloft to deal with the problems that I had.

Until I turned 18, I thought these experiences were just worries. Little did I know my constant worrying and bouts of sadness were actually diagnosable. These worries became what I am now aware are my anxieties. My inability to just relax stems from my anxiety. I was constantly "on" and in retrospect, my anxiety might have been a motivator in my competitiveness when it comes to school and my seeking validation.

I applied to several colleges in Florida, including UF, FSU, UNF, UCF, and Stetson. I waited anxiously for admission letters from December to March, and much to my surprise, I was accepted to every university that I applied to. I thought it was quite an accomplishment to do that since my older sister applied to just the one she was attending.

But I digress. During this time, my mental health was not getting better. I did not know how to deal with all of the emotions I was feeling. I felt overwhelmed by school, the club, college decisions, and my first relationship. I did not know where I wanted to go and I was growing impatient with my sisters and with my boyfriend—I kept getting snappier and meaner. I was miserable to be around most days.

By the time I had to decide where I wanted to go, my boyfriend had broken up with me. I thought this was all situational, and I was stressed about college and now my first *real* breakup. I never thought that I could be depressed or even thought I was "anxious." I just thought I was a teenage girl and every teenager felt these things when it came to college decisions and a first heartbreak.

My first heartbreak sent me down a terrible rabbit hole. I no longer wanted to go to any of my club's events—and I was president. I was disappointed with myself for not getting myself out of bed to go to events. I told people I was busy when I was just crying or attempting to sleep my days away. I barely ate. At this point I was 18 years old, 5'1", and less than 90 pounds. I was a stick and I was depressed.

Trigger warning for the passage below: suicide ideation.

One day, I think maybe in April of 2016, I was feeling my absolute worst—potentially the lowest point of my entire life. Now, thoughts of suicide are not necessarily "normal" but for someone in a depressed state, they can certainly seem to be the norm. You may have thoughts of suicide often, but not have any intention to act upon these thoughts.

Again, I would like to reiterate, this was the lowest I think I have ever been in my life. Certainly, in this state of mind, I often thought, "the world would be better off without me." I thought this without thinking about how my friends and family, and potentially just acquaintances, would feel about my death.

No one would care if you died. No one would care if you killed yourself. No one cares about you. You're better off dead. Just do everyone a favor, just kill yourself. Just die. Do it. These are things that Depression says to you when your mind is not in a good place. Depression is not kind and Depression does not discriminate.

While driving, I have thought about how easy it would be to just steer my car into the median. How easy it would be for me to angle my car *just right* in order to run into a tree. I have thought about how simply I have wanted to go by overdosing on painkillers. And I thought about drowning myself.

I am a huge advocate for self-care. One day, I was feeling really down in the dumps, and I decided I would take a bath. Usually, a nice, warm bubble bath makes me feel like I am being embraced and held.

But during this bath, my thoughts were being influenced by Depression. It told me to *just...just try. Try to kill yourself.* The idea of no longer being a part of the world is appealing when you feel like you are a waste of space. These feelings were incessant and made me think that the solution was to not exist—I did not want to feel like a burden any longer.

Granted, drowning is one of the most difficult ways to commit suicide. But morbid curiosity got the best of me. I kept trying to keep myself underwater, but if our body detects that we may be drowning, it knows better—and my body went into "fight" mode. I was literally fighting my own mind's desire to be dead, in order to survive.

Not only that, but my little sister began to wonder why I was taking such a long time in the bath. Typically, we would use the shower after one another around the same time each evening. But that evening, time had gotten away from me. She started knocking on the bathroom door.

"Hey, *Ate* Eileen, are you done yet?" I did not answer.

She began knocking again: "Helloooooo. Are you okay?" I was not okay.

I had to snap out of it. I did not realize what I was doing. I did not think this through. My family would be devastated. My sisters would be beyond heartbroken. It is the Three Stremming Sisters, the Tres Marias—not the two Stremming Sisters, not the Dos Marias (that definitely does not have the same ring to it!).

I am not saying that it is an easy thing—to "snap out of it." But hearing my sister's voice at this low point definitely got me out of my head and helped me to face my reality.

For a long time, I did not even tell anyone that I tried to drown myself, because it felt silly—drowning is so difficult to do successfully. So no one really knew but my therapists and me.

I have a family that loves me and I have friends that love me. Even though I do not feel like enough and sometimes I feel alone, I am not alone. I know that I am not alone and that always helps me feel a little grounded.

My mother and my sisters started worrying about me—my mother is actually the one who pushed in the right direction to begin going to therapy.

One day, it was getting to be too much for my mom to see how I was not myself. She sat me down and we had a conversation. I wrote down exactly what happened and have had this conversation saved in my notes because this was new—I think for the first time in my life, my mother and I had a real "TV show" heart-to-heart. We were talking about schools and my decision to attend UCF after months of wanting to attend FSU. I was quite sensitive during this time, which meant that many conversations that I would have would result in me crying.

Mom: Why are you crying? Stop crying. Eileen, stop crying I'm just trying to talk to you. Come here, I love you. Anger is a symptom of depression. I'm just trying to talk. You know you're depressed right? If you're alone, it's not going to get better. You can't help people if you're not okay first. I think you should start getting counseling with me. What do you think? Will you do that? It's taken me a long time to accept it, Eileen. You are my perfectionist, you always want to do the best that you can and that takes a toll on your mental health. You got more from me than you think. You're stubborn and you're sad like me. That's why you always want to sleep and not eat. I know, Eileen, it took me a long time to accept it. I'm sick in my head, it's all in my head, but it's a sickness just like heart disease. I'm sick.

Me: …yeah that's why it's a mental illness.

Mom, holding me: You need to get help, Eileen. I want you to get better before going to college and you're doing your own thing. You have the rest of your life, but I want you to get better as soon as possible. I denied it for so long and I don't want you to go through that.

Me: Okay.

Mom: Okay, you'll get help?

Me, wiping my tears, sniffling: I guess.

Mom: You'll get better and you'll know what you want to do.

Me: I guess so.

Mom: What do you want to eat? Do you want to order something?

Me: I'm not hungry.

Mom: Eileen, you need to eat something. You're not eating.

Me: I know.

Mom: Go see a movie with someone. Go out tonight, find a friend, don't be sad and don't cry tonight. I'll give you my card. Buy food.

Me: Okay.

Mom: So we're gonna get you help, okay?

Me: Okay.

Mom: I love you so much, stop trying to live up to people's expectations of you. Do what you want and take your time and take care of yourself. It's your life, Eileen.

To hear from my own mother that I should seek professional help for my mental health—an Asian mother, who are infamous for rarely saying "I love you" outright to begin with—was new, especially when I didn't even believe there was anything wrong with me. I started going to therapy right after my mom and I talked about my stresses and anxieties.

While we've made some gains in my family, we are not where I would like us to ultimately be just yet. We have got a ways to go, but with our best foot forward, I am thankful that we are going in the right direction.

Lessons & Takeaways:

- We are our own biggest enemies sometimes.
- It takes a little bit of a push from those who love us to start on a path that is good for us.
- You are loved more than you know.
- You are not only your ethnicity, you are not only your grades, and you are more than your traumas.
- You are who you are because of what you have been through. Grow through what you go through.

Chapter 2:
Same Illness, Different Reactions

———

"You guys don't have any idea how lucky you guys are," family members have told my sisters and me from an early age.

We are the first generation of our family to be born and raised in the United States. Our struggles are nowhere near similar to what our parents, grandparents, and aunts and uncles went through. We have never undervalued their experiences nor been ungrateful for our life here.

This difference in our upbringings, though, meant our mental problems are not understood as clearly as we would like them to be. Our family has always been incredibly hardworking and we have never been unappreciative of the fact that we are in the United States today.

But the idea of mental illness is not quite understood and can be disregarded easily because we have had "bigger things to worry about."

It is important to realize that even within the same family, experiences can be unique. My little sister's mental health journey is a little different especially when it comes to my family's response.

In August of 2016, while I was off to start college in a new city, Eliza was also getting a brand-new start. She packed her bags and moved across the country to live with our family in San Diego, California. My aunt on my mother's side took in my sister. For the first time in her life, at 15, she was going to be separated from our mother, our older sister, and me.

I thought that Eliza was incredibly strong and brave for leaving all of the friends she had ever known to start a new school and start an entirely new chapter. However, I did not think about how all of this would affect her mental health.

Her sophomore year, she was riddled with anxiety as she started her new school. When my aunt dropped her off on her first day of school, she was overwhelmed by thoughts such as, "How am I going to make new friends? How am I going to get used to all of this? I am in a whole new place, I'm scared."

After her first day, she called my older sister and me crying about how nervous she was. Even as her sister, I had not thought about her potential anxiety regarding picking up, leaving her life behind and starting anew.

My little sister has always been the "social butterfly" among the three of us. She has never had problems making friends, but that did not mean she could not also be overcome by the same kind of anxiety that I have.

On the bright side, she did not struggle making friends upon switching schools; she made two friends almost immediately and went to a beginning-of-the-year school dance with them.

Yet within two weeks of being at a new school, my little sister was cyber-bullied. A non-traceable number texted her, "For being at EHS for two weeks, you're lowkey a hoe."

It broke my heart knowing I could not be there to comfort her and I could not help her do anything. I was not her confidant that was right down the hall anymore and we would have to deal with our mental health problems by ourselves.

My sister ended up finding out who her bully was—and that the antagonist took the time to download an app to text her anonymously. Even though this affected her, she realized she has to be more careful about who she chooses to be her friends.

Eliza returned home to Florida in the summer of 2017, and upon her arrival home, she attempted to discuss her mental health problems with my mother and asked if she could get help and find a therapist. But, much to her surprise, she was almost immediately brushed off.

"Therapy?" my mother questioned. "Do you have money for that?" As previously stated, we have always had some financial problems, even though it has always seemed like we are well off. My mother's response left my sister and me somewhat confused, given that my mother pushed me toward getting professional help.

This was frustrating because Eliza lived in California and my mom did not get to see Eliza's daily routine or how similar her exhaustion was to mine in 2015 and 2016.

Upon returning to California for school in the fall of 2017, Eliza started having problems with a girl in her new friend group. She saw my sister as a threat and began bullying Eliza for being friendly with her boyfriend. This ex-friend started spreading rumors at the end of their junior year. This, in addition to her existing depression and anxiety, left my sister in a poor spot mentally.

Eliza did not really share with me or our older sister that this girl was really getting to her, so we did not really know.

In the fall of 2018, as Eliza was entering her senior year of high school, she wound up in the same group of friends as her bully again and tensions were high. Her bully kept starting drama and adding unnecessary stress to her life, which created a lot of strife and caused my sister to have many, many breakdowns.

My sister went without professional help—since my mother's disapproval was enough to stop her from seeking it—until right after one of Eliza's high school classmates committed suicide. Mental health professionals were on campus giving presentations for suicide prevention and making it known that there are text-lines and hotlines for suicide. There were preventative measures being taken by her high school. There was a form that made it easy to talk to a mental health professional at her high school that she filled out.

Within that week, she was interviewed by professionals regarding her mental health. My sister and I are relatively open when it comes to discussing our mental state, so she told the LMHC (Licensed Mental Health Counselor) everything—all of the sadness and lack of motivation—she had been feeling and unloaded all of the problems and stresses she had. The LMHC was only on campus for a few months and so Eliza was referred to outpatient treatment for talk therapy. So until December of 2018, Eliza did not go to therapy.

Finally, at 17, she was diagnosed with anxiety and depression. Eliza did not want to openly share with our family all that she had been feeling, for fear of being judged or brushed off again. So the LMHC shared the news with my family on her behalf. Reactions were not as similar to my diagnosis as we had hoped they would be.

My grandmother, who came to the United States in 1998, wants and always hopes for the best for her grandchildren, and wants us in the United States to thrive and be successful. So, being sensitive is often not seen as a positive quality because no one wants to deal with crying spells and the over-emotionality of a young girl, plus we should always stay strong regardless.

My grandmother told Eliza, "Be strong, you don't want your tears to go to waste. Save your tears for times that are hard or for my funeral." My grandmother is one of the strongest people I know, never wavering when something might bother her, and we love her so much. I have always respected my grandmother's will to continue on. But this sadness is something that we feel she understands because she has always worked so hard and always moves forward. There is often not time to be upset.

And another family member commented, "Oh, she's just copying Eileen."

It was frustrating for both of us that they would say those things. I hated that they discounted what Eliza was going through and said that she was copying me. The inheritability of depression and anxiety for me was just as likely for her.

The Anxiety and Depression Association of America (ADAA) has noted, "While depression affects all ages and both genders, girls are more likely to develop depression during adolescence."

Several people attributed her lack of motivation, inability to feed herself, and constant want to sleep to being a lazy teenager, and her crying spells to being sensitive, when it was honestly much more than being sensitive.

Depression can manifest in several ways, and our cases were pretty similar in our desire to avoid everything by sleeping and to go without eating.

It is extremely unfortunate that our experiences with our family's reaction regarding our mental health were not the same, but it can be hard to convey, "Hey, her mental health problems are just as valid as mine!" to everyone in the family.

My sisters and I are able to talk about everything and anything with each other; so the state of our mental health is not a topic that ever really goes unspoken.

When I was very depressed, some nights Eliza would sleep in my room when I was upset to make me feel less alone.

My sisters would always try to talk to me about what was going on in my head and we would just sit with each other and talk when we were feeling unwell.

While Eliza did not get this same treatment given that my older sister Erika and I lived on the other side of the country, we tried to always be available via FaceTime or phone call—but the result was not nearly the same.

Eliza felt like everyone was treating her unfairly and not at all like they treated and responded to me when they found out that I have depression and anxiety. It is unfair that I have gotten passes and people believe that my want to stay in bed is because of my depression, while Eliza's want to stay in bed is related to her teenage laziness.

Unfortunately, this understanding waxes and wanes. There has been more understanding towards Eliza's experiences, and less towards mine. They have not been as hard on Eliza, and I have been told to just stay busy to avoid getting sad.

We have both been told that therapy is unnecessary and that we do not really need to go.

While it is an overstatement to say everyone in my family does not understand, it can sometimes feel that way. We are still making strides to better Eliza's mental health and get my family on the same page so that we can both have our mental health issues be validated.

For now, Eliza is getting help and going to therapy, and we can only hope that we will be able to talk openly about our experiences and help our family understand that our struggles are a little different than theirs were.

Lessons & Takeaways:

- Every experience with mental health is unique.
- Outward appearances do not always match inner turmoil.
- Everyone has something going on, and we might not always know it.
- Ask about what is going on. Be genuine about your intentions and care.
- We must be gentle with ourselves and those around us.

Eliza wants people that read her story to know:

- Sometimes these experiences can lead us to grow thicker skin.
- Bullies are insecure and want other people to feel the same as they do.
- Rise above the pettiness; do not stoop to those levels.

Chapter 3:
Out Of Sight, Out Of Mind

Regarding the mental health stigma—especially in families with immigrant parents—talking about mental health problems is incredibly difficult. According to the American Psychological Association, Asian Americans often underutilize mental health services. This may be due to the rate of assimilation and adaptation to culture.

Asian American Psychological Association (AAPA) Member Matthew Miller, PhD, Associate Professor of Counseling Psychology at the University of Maryland, College Park, studied the generational differences conflict between immigrant parents and their children that may arise due to acculturation and found that in general, children adapt to the culture of the United States more quickly than their immigrant parents.

There is a huge discrepancy between generations when it comes to understanding mental health and the problems that are associated with it. There are so many differences between first-generation immigrants and the first generation to be born and raised in the new country. The struggles are different and incomparable, which means there are cultural barriers and so many misunderstandings.

The journey with mental health problems is never an easy trek to make. The beginning is especially rough—taking the first steps on any journey is difficult, especially when people you had hoped would be supportive of it begin to become barriers themselves.

Upon starting your mental health journey, worrying about others' opinions can be difficult, and it can be even more difficult to disregard them. If people you can talk to about a plethora of things cannot come to understand your mental health problems, this can be a difficult journey to face alone. And no one wants to take on anything alone.

Relationships between parents and children can be hard to navigate and I think that variations in our childhoods can make all the difference. Generational differences including what is taboo and what is not can add barriers to a relationship. Add growing up in different countries to the mix and it can seem as if your parent is actually a stranger.

Loya, Reddy, and Hinshaw found that South Asians are more likely to stigmatize mental illness than Caucasians. The stigma in Asian cultures makes it hard to seek professional help or even talk about mental health problems; the cultural difference makes it especially difficult to discuss if you are the child of Asian immigrants because they have worked so hard for us to be able to live the lives that we are fortunate to have.

Justin Nguyen is a first-generation to be born and raised in the United States. His parents came from Vietnam when they were about 11 or 12 years old. Similar to other children of immigrants, a few that will be shared later, Justin is grateful for his parents and has a good relationship with them. However, in his experience he has found it very hard to talk about mental health or anything regarding emotions with them.

Justin shares that "…there is this disconnect…I do not know if it is because of the culture from when they were raised back in Vietnam, and over here in the States, but the way that I have a relationship with my parents is very different from the way that my American friends with their parents. My girlfriend… the way she is able to talk to her mom is completely different than the way I am able to talk to my dad or even my mother."

Unfortunately, having immigrant parents can mean that the chances they took in order to come to the United States are held over our heads. The mindset that many immigrant parents have, as Justin notes, is often, "That should not be a problem for you. If we were able to do it, why can't you?"

The comparison is so hard to make because we were fortunate enough to have been born and raised here in the United States. Our experiences growing up are not the same as our parents' so our struggles will be different.

Justin notes that he has seen it among his peers with immigrant parents where they discount our side of things.

His parents, he says, are very old school. "We came over here, we left everything, we gave you this life, this amazing life, this amazing house, we helped you get through college, you're telling me that you're struggling with not finding a career? How does that make any sense?"

In high school, Justin was a big soccer athlete. He says that during one of the lowest points of his life, he felt as if he could not talk to his parents about it. He says he tried to communicate with his parents about things but often felt like they could never understand.

In junior year, he broke his leg. Breaking his leg sent him on a different life path, which he says really changed his life. His father had been very supportive of his soccer career, which was a bonding point for them. Since his dad loved soccer, he felt like his dad would not understand how he felt about the incident.

Justin used to be a soccer star with scholarships and the opportunity to play soccer in college. This was an achievement his parents were proud of. But suddenly, it was gone. He never felt like he could talk to his mother about how much this affected him.

I have tried to bond over my achievements with my mother. I know firsthand how hard it can be to discuss certain topics with Asian parents. My mother used to boast about my and my sisters' achievements to her friends.

It is somewhat common among Asian parents to compare their children's achievements to those of the children of their friends. To lose something that made his parents proud affected Justin more than his parents would ever come to know. Sometimes, you can talk about things with your parents, but it never reaches any resolution.

"I think that is the whole thing. It is like, a lot of times parents say one thing, but they act a different way. And I feel like that is something my parents have done, I have definitely seen it with other parents too," Justin says.

In Justin's experience, his mother compared him with another Vietnamese student and felt competitive regarding his academic success—she told Justin that he had "lost" to another Vietnamese student. Justin was not as invested as his mother was and never viewed himself as that dedicated to academics, so he did not mind "losing."

Our parents would talk about achievements for hours, but the mental health of their children is something that Asian parents would *never* boast about. In fact, it is something that you would rarely hear conversations about among immigrant parents.

Justin has found it harder being both a man and the child of an immigrant because there is also a stigma attached to men discussing emotional problems. He noted that it is difficult being a guy and saying out loud, "I am depressed," or even "I am feeling sad." But he is hopeful and says it is starting to change because of celebrities.

> **"As more and more celebrities come out with their mental health problems, it helps normalize the idea of mental health problems little by little. When it is in the mainstream media, Justin thinks, we as Americans will adapt to the normalization."**

He believes that immigrants will be one of the last groups to be understanding because "if it's not physical, and if you can't see it, then it's out of mind. It is hard to convince your parents that you have depression or even just have them accept it."

The idea that if you cannot see it is difficult because a mental illness is just that—unseen by the human eye. It is mental. We are able to see the effects of mental illness, but we will never be able to actually see it like we can see a broken leg.

For Justin, he has a hard time talking to his parents about mental health, even though he wants to. It is hard for his parents to be convinced that depression really, truly exists. If the barrier does not break, then some parents will not understand and these mental health problems will come off as excuses—and not as an illness.

In immigrant families, the idea that you are mentally ill is not understood completely. So it is our job to help our families and friends learn and attempt to understand. The stigma makes it even more difficult for children attempting to even discuss mental health problems with their parents.

Moreover, Vicki Zakrzewski, PhD, education director of the Greater Good Science Center, notes that in general, "…our society labels men as unable to feel or connect to the same degree that women can." However, these labels are simply untrue.

We often do not cultivate and allow men to be as open with their feelings as women can be. The gender role, according to Levant et al. (2003), requires men to achieve dominant and aggressive roles.

We stigmatize men, thus not allowing them the space to discuss what they are feeling. This further illustrates to and embeds in men that it is out of sight, and out of mind. It is unfair that we do not grant them the opportunity to discuss what they are feeling, because it might be out of sight, but it is not out of mind.

Stanford professor Judy Chu wrote *When Boys Become Boys* and has found that it is culture as opposed to nature that suppresses boys' social and emotional skills.

The American Psychological Association has found, "Males are the most socially vulnerable and at greatest risk for health disparities." Unfortunately, this forced gender role has its consequences in different ways—men are up to four times as likely to commit suicide.

Several of these problems are not only due to personal decisions, but also due to society and its influences. Studies of men's health have found that they are less likely to seek medical attention and get help—thus making them more vulnerable to illnesses and mental health problems.

Justin was one of the only males that was okay discussing his experience with me. It was difficult to find men for this book that were willing to discuss their experiences with mental health. It is up to us to make it okay for not just minorities to discuss these issues, but for men.

Lessons & Takeaways:

- Men have mental health problems too.
- When someone is attempting to share sensitive information with you, do not brush it off.
- Immigrant parents, be more open and understanding and *please* stop comparing us to our own siblings or the children of your friends.
- Struggles are struggles despite how "good" it seems someone might have it.
- Talking about something that hurts does not mean we are ungrateful about other aspects of our lives.

Chapter 4:

There's A Need
To Bridge The Gap

Growing up in the United States with any semblance of an ethnic background can often pose difficulty for children of immigrants. Sometimes you might hear, "Go back to where you came from!" However, there is no "back" for children that were born in the States. This is just as much our country as it is for those who have been here for generations.

For Sigiana, she grew up in a very traditional Albanian household, which she says was "...more traditional than many of my Albanian friends."

She notes that as she and her sister grew up, they had to teach their parents how assimilate to American culture and accept certain parts of it.

This is not uncommon. Immigrants often are caught in between cultures and they often want to keep as much of their culture as possible in their everyday life. Sigiana notes that her parents' initial reaction to moving here was to preserve their culture as much as possible.

Similar to Sigiana, I have seen my family attempting to preserve a lot of our culture. While everyone in our family has assimilated well, we have not lost our connection to our heritage. It is alive and kicking in our connection to the language, through television and food.

She states, "It was difficult growing up and going to schools where everyone seemed to have this freedom and free will that I just didn't have. And as a child of an immigrant family who worked so hard to be here I could not really go against my parents because I had too much respect for them to shame them like that."

Children of immigrants often find themselves trying to live for themselves but also to please their parents. There is a common ambition among children of immigrants to succeed and to be the best that you can be, since our parents came to the States to better our lives.

This can often lead to a mutual and unspoken agreement that allows for good relationships that are not resentful, but more respectful of our parents, which some of our non-immigrant peers may not understand.

Sigiana says, "I'd like to say I have a good relationship with my parents because I love them so much and they are very loving and caring. But there are many things that I don't feel comfortable talking to them about, and to be honest they don't know about 10% of what goes on in my life and what I do."

Jessica Finney, University of Florida Doctor of Physical Therapy student, mentions that parents can help their children by "...providing a nonjudgmental place for their children to share their thoughts and feelings. Paying attention to see if their child is acting different and might be in the midst of a crisis. Understanding and maintaining boundaries. If possible, financially helping their children seek mental health counseling or psychiatry."

Moreover, while parents may provide space to talk about things, there is not always that trust. Sigiana states, "My mom always tells my sister and I that we can talk to her about things but deep down we know we can't tell her a majority of things about our lives because she would never approve and could never understand. There is always this barrier keeping us from actually being close."

It is not uncommon for mental health to be brushed off in immigrant families. These underlying issues tend to stay buried.

The same was true for Sigiana growing up. She notes, "Mental health problems were never really addressed in my family, I don't think my parents really understand that mental health is more than just a fleeting feeling, even though they try to."

There are several instances that children of immigrants can call on where a serious issue was not fully realized as a mental health problem.

There are common themes across cultures that have yet to accept that mental health is something that needs to be addressed.

In my own experience, I have found myself brushing off my problems or sadness, because it was not a big deal and I did not want to bother anyone with it.

Sigiana recalls: "I distinctly remember one time in the 5th grade I had been crying for a while and mustered up the courage to go to my mom and tell her I was sad. She handed me a bottle of Coke and told me to go sit outside and get some air (this actually kind of helped)." And it is instances like this that can make it difficult to try to muster up the courage to talk to our parents when we feel off.

I know that if I spend more than one day feeling unmotivated and wanting to sleep all day, my mother has said things such as, "Just go outside and sit by the pool and you will feel better." While my relationship with my mother is slightly different than what my peers go through, I have found that it is hard to really tell my mom what I am feeling.

Sigiana also notes that in college, her sister experienced severe suicidal problems that she did not tell their family about for years. And when she did, it was not a topic addressed for longer than the span of that one conversation. She says she knows that they try to understand, but they just do not see the depth of the problem like she and her sister do.

Since becoming a psychology major, and graduating with her Bachelor's in psychology, she says, "I know my parents view it as something more serious now, but I still do not think they understand it. I know that mental health problems are something they have experienced themselves but they just do not know how to explain it."

Unfortunately, the culture that she grew up in has made these matters private. Upon being asked about the state of her sister's mental health, she replies, "She has had problems in the past and I'm pretty sure she's currently facing some too… I would like to think I am very close with my sister but we will not tell each other about our problems until they are over. Sometimes it is because we don't want to stress each other out, other times it is because we just don't know how to talk to each other. I think we are just so used to dealing with things by ourselves that it's hard to admit something is wrong and sometimes it is even hard to understand what it is we are feeling."

The stigma surrounding therapy as check-ins or even as a means to feel somewhat "okay" is still very prevalent. She states, "I do not think therapy is necessarily frowned upon in my family, but I do think my parents think it is something for severe cases and not just 'for any teenage girl.' I still think that there is still some stigma about how relatives might view them if they knew their daughter was in therapy."

She shares that she still does not have a good way to cope with her emotions. She says she tries to keep herself from getting too into her head and from overthinking, adding, "I try to distract myself and keep busy. When it gets bad I reach out to certain friends for comfort and guidance but other than that I still keep to myself."

I think that it is completely okay for people to keep to themselves as they see fit, but hope that everyone knows that it is okay to talk about what you are currently going through. And it is okay to feel sad for a bit. Distractions divert you from what the real issue at hand is.

As for alternative ways to deal with these issues, in her culture, she says there really are none. It is typical for everyone to just kind of deal with their own problems and learn not to show them.

But on that note, she says, "I would tell my younger self to put myself first more and take more chances, reach out to more people and do not be afraid to be vulnerable. Addressing things and fixing them are uncomfortable but it needs to be done, better sooner than later."

It is common to keep these kinds of issues to oneself in immigrant families. There is this want to not be a burden, so you carry it all on your own shoulders. However, I want to let people know that it is really okay to talk about what is going on. In fact, it is incredibly important to talk about what you are going through. You do not have to walk any path alone.

In fact, building a support system is the best way to combat the lone journey. Regarding support systems, Jessica Finney adds: "Having a support system, for me at least, plays a big role in helping me to continue using the coping skills that I've learned through counseling. I understand it can be hard to acknowledge that your family might not be that support system for you. We're trained to think that our family is a built-in support system from birth, but at the end of the day if your family isn't providing the support you need for your mental health, having a group to support you is important. I think a lot of people would feel like this is 'replacing' their family, or it's a betrayal. It doesn't mean going no contact (unless that's the move for that particular person) or that your family is no longer in your life. It just means you realize that you need to have a support system since your family either isn't capable of being that for you or still has steps to take to be that support system you need."

While I am so incredibly fortunate to have my sisters' support throughout my journey, I know that this is not always something that all people have. Our friends can become our support system. Whoever we consider our loved ones can be our support system, as long as we let them.

There is a mental gap that needs to be addressed in normalizing discussing the state of our mental health in addition to just being comfortable talking about what is going on. We are afraid of being burdensome or annoying, but when people love you, they are more than willing to listen to what is going on.

Lessons & Takeaways:

- Immigrant parents and children often have a different relationship built on the idea that we all want to be successful.
- Parents can provide support through creating nonjudgmental spaces or giving financial means to seek professional help.
- Check in with your siblings. You do not have to wait until a problem is over to talk about what is bothering you.
- Distractions can be good, but they do not work for everyone. Addressing the true problem leads to progress.
- You do not have to walk your journey alone! You can choose who is in your support system. It does not have to be only your family.

count their own personal responsibility, and finding
ys to advocate and educate themselves. There are many
portunities to help if we help look for them."

Education regarding mental illness is something that
eryone is able to participate in. Simply by reading this
ok, you are educating yourself about what people have
n through. Lending an ear to a friend can teach you a lot
re than you might realize.

Upon being asked why it's important to break down the
ma regarding mental health, Jessica Finney had this to
"Struggling with mental health is incredibly common
people are afraid to talk about it. Dealing with mental
lth struggles is hard enough without feeling stigmatized,
ne, or weak. Breaking down the stigma would make it
er to seek care. Education is power!"

f we keep the conversation open and educate our friends
family, then we are helping to break the stigma regarding
tal health.

n line with education, we need to be able to recognize
s that are often associated with some of the more prevalent
tal illnesses. There are many mental illnesses, but for
ake of educational purposes, a few common ones are
d below.

Part II:
BE ACCOUNTABLE

Chapter 5:
Educate to Adv

Educate

Education and prevention are the bes
If we do not understand mental health
to reconstruct society's idea of it? Mer
that many people do not understand
through issues themselves.

So in order to be empathetic to oth
to realize that our experience is not t
We all go through different things. M
opportunities to constantly be bette
fellow humans, so that we can help
journeys. We have to speak out for t
their voices will not be heard in or

Sherry Warner, a certified mental
says, "Individuals motivated to he
health can help the cause by bei

stig
say
but
hea
alo
easi

and
mer

sign
mer
the
liste

These signs and symptoms are from the National Institute of Mental Health (NIMH):

Anxiety Disorders
Prevalence rate: 19.1% of adults (aged 18 and older)
General Anxiety Disorder, one might:
- Feel restless, wound-up, or on edge
- Be easily fatigued
- Have difficulty concentrating; mind may go blank
- Be irritable
- Have muscle tension
- Experience difficulty controlling feelings of worry
- Have sleep problems, such as difficulty falling or staying asleep, restlessness, or unsatisfying sleep

Panic Disorder; During a panic attack, one might have:
- Heart palpitations, a pounding heartbeat, or an accelerated heartrate
- Sweating
- Trembling or shaking
- Sensations of shortness of breath, smothering, or choking
- Feelings of impending doom
- Feelings of being out of control

Bipolar Disorder

Prevalence rate: 2.8% of adults (aged 18 and older)

In a manic state, one might:

- Feel very "up," "high," or elated
- Have a lot of energy
- Have increased activity levels
- Feel "jumpy" or "wired"
- Have trouble sleeping
- Become more active than usual
- Talk really fast about a lot of different things
- Be agitated, irritable, or "touchy"
- Feel like their thoughts are going very fast
- Think they can do a lot of things at once
- Do risky things, like spend a lot of money or have reckless sex

And in a depressed state, one might:

- Feel very sad, down, empty, or hopeless
- Have very little energy
- Have decreased activity levels
- Have trouble sleeping; they may sleep too little or too much
- Feel like they can't enjoy anything
- Feel worried and empty
- Have trouble concentrating
- Forget things a lot
- Eat too much or too little
- Feel tired or "slowed down"
- Think about death or suicide

Part II:
BE ACCOUNTABLE

Chapter 5:
Educate to Advocate

———

Educate

Education and prevention are the best cures for any ailment. If we do not understand mental health, how are we supposed to reconstruct society's idea of it? Mental health is something that many people do not understand unless they are going through issues themselves.

So in order to be empathetic to others' experiences, we need to realize that our experience is not the universal experience. We all go through different things. Moreover, we need to seek opportunities to constantly be better to ourselves and to our fellow humans, so that we can help each other on our life journeys. We have to speak out for those that might feel as if their voices will not be heard in order to save lives.

Sherry Warner, a certified mental health first aid instructor, says, "Individuals motivated to help de-stigmatize mental health can help the cause by being hopeful, taking into account their own personal responsibility, and finding ways to advocate and educate themselves. There are many opportunities to help if we help look for them."

Education regarding mental illness is something that everyone is able to participate in. Simply by reading this book, you are educating yourself about what people have been through. Lending an ear to a friend can teach you a lot more than you might realize.

Upon being asked why it's important to break down the stigma regarding mental health, Jessica Finney had this to say: "Struggling with mental health is incredibly common but people are afraid to talk about it. Dealing with mental health struggles is hard enough without feeling stigmatized, alone, or weak. Breaking down the stigma would make it easier to seek care. Education is power!"

If we keep the conversation open and educate our friends and family, then we are helping to break the stigma regarding mental health.

In line with education, we need to be able to recognize signs that are often associated with some of the more prevalent mental illnesses. There are many mental illnesses, but for the sake of educational purposes, a few common ones are listed below.

These signs and symptoms are from the National Institute of Mental Health (NIMH):

Anxiety Disorders

Prevalence rate: 19.1% of adults (aged 18 and older)

General Anxiety Disorder, one might:

- Feel restless, wound-up, or on edge
- Be easily fatigued
- Have difficulty concentrating; mind may go blank
- Be irritable
- Have muscle tension
- Experience difficulty controlling feelings of worry
- Have sleep problems, such as difficulty falling or staying asleep, restlessness, or unsatisfying sleep

Panic Disorder; During a panic attack, one might have:

- Heart palpitations, a pounding heartbeat, or an accelerated heartrate
- Sweating
- Trembling or shaking
- Sensations of shortness of breath, smothering, or choking
- Feelings of impending doom
- Feelings of being out of control

Bipolar Disorder

Prevalence rate: 2.8% of adults (aged 18 and older)

In a manic state, one might:

- Feel very "up," "high," or elated
- Have a lot of energy
- Have increased activity levels
- Feel "jumpy" or "wired"
- Have trouble sleeping
- Become more active than usual
- Talk really fast about a lot of different things
- Be agitated, irritable, or "touchy"
- Feel like their thoughts are going very fast
- Think they can do a lot of things at once
- Do risky things, like spend a lot of money or have reckless sex

And in a depressed state, one might:

- Feel very sad, down, empty, or hopeless
- Have very little energy
- Have decreased activity levels
- Have trouble sleeping; they may sleep too little or too much
- Feel like they can't enjoy anything
- Feel worried and empty
- Have trouble concentrating
- Forget things a lot
- Eat too much or too little
- Feel tired or "slowed down"
- Think about death or suicide

Depression

Prevalence rate: 7.1% or 17.3 million adults (aged 18 and older)

Symptoms may include:

- Feeling sad, irritable, or anxious
- Feeling empty, hopeless, guilty, or worthless
- Loss of pleasure in usually enjoyed hobbies or activities, including sex
- Fatigue and decreased energy, feeling listless
- Trouble concentrating, remembering details, and making decisions
- Not being able to sleep, or sleeping too much, or waking too early
- Eating too much or not wanting to eat at all, possibly with unplanned weight gain or loss
- Thoughts of death, suicide or suicide attempts
- Aches or pains, headaches, cramps, or digestive problems without a clear physical cause and/or that do not ease even with treatment

Personality Disorders

Prevalence rate: All Personality Disorders: 9.1% (1.9% with Borderline Personality Disorder)

Important to note: The comorbidity rate of bipolar personality disorder with another mental disorder is extremely high, at 84.5%.

Past Year Co-morbidity of Personality Disorders with Other Core Disorders Among U.S. Adults Data from National Comorbidity Survey - Replication (NCS-R)[1]		
	Any Personality Disorder (%)	Borderline (%)
Any Anxiety Disorder	52.4	60.5
Any Mood Disorder	24.1	34.3
Any Impulse Control Disorder	23.2	49.0
Any Substance Use Disorder	22.6	38.2
Any Disorder	67.0	84.5

The National Institute of Mental Health states:

People with borderline personality disorder may experience mood swings and display uncertainty about how they see themselves and their role in the world. As a result, their interests and values can change quickly.

People with borderline personality disorder also tend to view things in extremes, such as all good or all bad. Their opinions of other people can also change quickly. An individual who is seen as a friend one day may be considered an enemy or traitor the next. These shifting feelings can lead to intense and unstable relationships.

Other Symptoms of BPD MAY include:

- Efforts to avoid real or imagined abandonment, such as rapidly initiating intimate (physical or emotional) relationships or cutting off communication with someone in anticipation of being abandoned

- A pattern of intense and unstable relationships with family, friends, and loved ones, often swinging from extreme closeness and love (idealization) to extreme dislike or anger (devaluation)
- Distorted and unstable self-image or sense of self
- Impulsive and often dangerous behaviors, such as spending sprees, unsafe sex, substance abuse, reckless driving, and binge eating.
  Please note: If these behaviors occur primarily during a period of elevated mood or energy, they may be signs of a mood disorder—not borderline personality disorder
- Self-harming behavior, such as cutting
- Recurring thoughts of suicidal behaviors or threats
- Intense and highly changeable moods, with each episode lasting from a few hours to a few days
- Chronic feelings of emptiness
- Inappropriate, intense anger or problems controlling anger
- Difficulty trusting, which is sometimes accompanied by irrational fear of other people's intentions
- Feelings of dissociation, such as feeling cut off from oneself, seeing oneself from outside one's body, or feelings of unreality

Post-Traumatic Stress Disorder (PTSD) *Prevalence rate: 3.6% of adults (aged 18 and older)*

Symptoms may include:

(1) Re-experiencing symptom

- Flashbacks—reliving the trauma over and over, including physical symptoms like a racing heart or sweating
- Bad dreams
- Frightening thoughts

(1) Avoidance symptom

- Staying away from places, events, or objects that are reminders of the experience
- Avoiding thoughts or feelings related to the traumatic event

(2) Arousal and reactivity symptoms

- Being easily startled
- Feeling tense or "on edge"
- Having difficulty sleeping, and/or having angry outbursts

(2) Cognition and mood symptoms:

- Trouble remembering key features of the traumatic event
- Negative thoughts about oneself or the world
- Distorted feelings like guilt or blame
- Loss of interest in enjoyable activities

Advocate

By educating ourselves and normalizing conversations regarding mental health, we then make it okay for others to speak about their experiences with mental health problems. By educating ourselves, we then also begin to realize that our reckless use of words such as "depressed," "anxious," or "bipolar" are off base. This paves the way for us to become advocates.

Additionally, by reading about actual experiences regarding mental health problems, this gives you insight into the minds of those that you might not otherwise understand. My friend Lainey who often speaks out regarding her mental health and her experiences, says we can help to break the stigma if we keep talking.

"There are always going to be people who disagree or just do not care, the point is not to change people's minds, it is to inspire other people to stand up and speak out as well," she says.

If we learn what common disorders might entail, then we can begin to realize that our sadness that might last a day is not synonymous with a mental health disorder that results in a loss of interest in activities that used to make you happy.

Our butterflies might not be equivalent to incessant worrying. Anxiety is actually constantly worrying and all-consuming. We all tend to feel a bit of anxiety—and while anxiety can sometimes motivate us, to invalidate someone with an Anxiety Disorder because you, too, may have some anxiety when speaking in public or going into a job interview is unfair.

And when the sun is shining one moment and begins to downpour an hour later, the weather is, by absolutely no means, bipolar.

It can be frustrating when people use these words to describe much simpler feelings. I have found myself telling people, "Hey, that is actually insensitive. The weather is not bipolar though it is a little unpredictable."

When we can realize that some trials that people go through are often not of their own choice, we can be more sensitive to their experiences. Once we know these things, we can speak on the behalf of our peers and our loved ones and become advocates for them.

Additionally, if we can do our best to prevent emergencies that may result in a Baker Act,* then something is being done correctly. Ajai R. Singh M.D. has this to say about prevention:

"The first goal of medicine is to see to it that no one has to reach a hospital or a clinic. This is what I mean by prevention. [Technically called primary prevention; not of course ruling out the importance of secondary prevention (early detection and prompt treatment) and tertiary prevention (restoring function and reducing disability)]"

If we are able to recognize the signs after educating ourselves, then we can not only help prevent possible suicides but begin to speak out on behalf of those that are not always able to speak out. Education is one of the first steps that result in change.

*The Baker Act is a Florida law that enables families and loved ones to provide emergency mental health services and temporary detention for people who are impaired because of their mental illness, and who are unable to determine their needs for treatment (UFHealth.org)**.**

Lessons & Takeaways:

- We need to take it upon ourselves to educate ourselves.
- Your experience is not the universal experience, so be more empathetic.
- We can be better by teaching ourselves.
- Be more careful with your word choices, it can come off as insensitive, even if you do not intend it to.
- Use your voice, even if you are not experiencing any mental health problems, for everyone who might be afraid to speak out.
- Immigrant families, we can do our parts and make it okay for all of us to get help. There is no shame in educating ourselves and also making an example of what is acceptable—going to therapy being one of those things!

Chapter 6:
Holding Ourselves Accountable

———

"Education and advocacy are crucial for breaking down the stigma regarding mental health, quite simply because lives are at stake. People have died, are dying, and will continue to die, if they are afraid or ashamed to communicate the depths of despair they feel that precedes the thought to take their own lives. Community members, friends, and loved ones need to know how to recognize the signs, what to say and do, and just as important—what not to say and what not to do. "

—SHERRY WARNER, CERTIFIED MENTAL HEALTH FIRST AID INSTRUCTOR

By holding ourselves accountable in how we treat people, then we will be able to do just that—recognize the signs, know what to say or do, and what not to say or do.

In the previous chapter, signs for a diagnosis for anxiety, bipolar disorder, depression, personality disorders, and PTSD were noted. In this chapter, the distinction becomes somewhat blurred because we will attempt to dig into the symptoms of common disorders (namely anxiety and depression) and attempt to picture how someone with a mental illness might act because coping mechanisms are not always the same. Additionally, some mental disorders may result in masks that are put on to make it seem as if everything is fine when (spoiler!) things are not okay.

It is important to note that there are people with mental illnesses who are high functioning and may not act how we imagine someone who might be anxious or depressed to act.

Anxiety

Anxiety differentiates itself from regular anxious thoughts because it is diagnosed if a person has three or more symptoms and worry that is difficult to control more days than not for at least six months.

Sometimes someone with GAD may over-prepare because the uncertainty of everyday life may be incredibly overwhelming. Additionally, they attempt to plan and avoid situations (potentially social experiences, which may be related to social anxiety) that might cause more anxiety.

Anxiety can manifest in the form of stomach problems, fatigue, insomnia, and restlessness. It can also cause someone to be irritable.

Scientifically, stress receptors are activated because anxiety activates our fight-or-flight responses and thus our sympathetic nervous system is suddenly on. Our amygdala—responsible for emotional processing—sends a signal to our hypothalamus, which communicates with other parts of our body that control involuntary responses such as our heartbeat and breathing. Our hypothalamus activates the sympathetic nervous which results in stress hormones being released, thus resulting in our fight-or-flight reaction. This hyper-vigilance can cause potential irritability.

Neil Hughes is a comedian, author, and physicist who has lived with anxiety for years. He has said, "I ended up living with quite horrible anxiety. I couldn't sleep, I couldn't relax, I couldn't enjoy life at all. And unfortunately my reaction was to worry about it…which just made it worse."

Speaking from experience, I often have a hard time saying "no" for fear of upsetting someone. I have often hoped that someone would cancel plans with me or tell me I no longer have to do something that I previously agreed to. This can lead to overextending myself when I need to take care of myself. Make sure your friends know that it is okay if they say "no."

Here are a few things you should *probably* not say to someone with anxiety, and what you can say instead.

1. "You have to calm down."

This can be pretty irritating because if they are anxious about something, chances are they are not able to simply calm down. This is pretty similar to telling someone to "just stop" feeling whatever they are feeling. And oftentimes, this anxiety is not completely controllable—hence why they might be a little on edge. Someone might not understand their anxious feelings or how to relieve the anxiety that they might have.

→ **Try being understanding. You can simply ask, "Is there something on your mind that might be overwhelming you?" and allow the conversation to be open enough to create a safe environment for them to talk about what might be making them anxious. And listen.**

2. "Chill out." or "Jeez, relax."

It's not that simple for people to simply turn off their brains and not feel so "on" about their worries. It is difficult to deal with them, and very difficult to simply chill out about something.

→ **Try simply being there and allowing them to be anxious, but remind them that they can manage these worries more easily. Potentially, offer a solution that may include meditation or mindfulness…or simply taking a break or a breath to "chill out."**

3. "You're overreacting," or "You shouldn't worry so much."

Odds are, they probably are not putting on a show for you. Anxiety can exacerbate things that may be small for someone without all-consuming worry. No one wants to let one little thought take control and bother them. It is not that simple. Being told you are overreacting could potentially cause an anxiety attack—which, to an outsider, may seem like another overreaction. But imagine thinking that something might go wrong and it is the only thing you are able to think about—even if it might be "small." Then someone tells you you're overreacting, so you might get upset with yourself for feeling that way. This can affect someone more than you know. We need to be careful with our words.

→ Try **"Take your time, your worries are not dumb. I know you can't control it."**

4. "It's not a big deal."

To you, this might be true. But to them, these worries are overwhelming and it is a big deal to them. Please, please, do not invalidate someone's experience because you do not understand. Be empathetic, try to put yourself in their shoes. We are not mind readers—so we will never know how someone's thoughts are affecting them. It can be hard for some people to deal with their own thoughts—and to say "it's not a big deal" may make them feel like they should not feel the way they do.

→ Try **"I know this seems like a lot; how can I help?"**

Depression

When we think about depression, we should not imagine *Eeyore*—*Eeyore* seems consistently sad and has dysthymia, which is a mild but long-term depression—but we should realize that depression can look like a lot of things.

Depression is different from sadness or grief because there is mixed feelings of happiness in times of grief whereas depression is the loss of pleasure in daily life. It is normal to be upset after a loss of a relationship, job, or death of a loved one.

Additionally, feelings of worthlessness are often associated with depression whereas when grieving, one's self-esteem is not affected. It is important to note, however, that what brings on grief can lead to major depression. Additionally, with depression, suicidal ideation may occur or just general thoughts of death are common.

Depression can look like weight gain or weight loss—and it is not related to dieting. Depression can look like one of your happy, busy friends. Or it can be your friend that stays in bed all weekend. Depression wears different masks.

Sometimes, depression does not look like sadness because it is quite easy to put a mask on and attempt to go through the motions of life. I have been told, on more than one occasion, something along the lines of: "I love how you're always smiling! It's so contagious. You're so happy!"

I hear this when I am honestly very, very sad. It becomes easy to just pretend like all is well so that you do not go around worrying your loved ones. But the fact of the matter is, my depression has resulted in me losing 25 pounds, and it makes me feel like I have to constantly be moving so that I do not become sad.

If I do not keep busy, I have absolutely no problem staying in bed and sleeping my day away. It is really easy for me to go out and smile and pretend like everything is okay. I do not necessarily enjoy the activities that keep me busy, but I find that I do not sit in self-hatred if I am busy.

Here are a few things you should *probably* not say to someone with depression, and what you can say instead.

1. "Don't be sad! You have so much to be happy about!"

So many factors go into one's depression. The American Psychiatric Association says, "Being sad is not the same as having depression." Someone with depression did not wake up one day and just decide, "Let me be sad today." Sometimes they try to wake up and tell themselves that they want to be happy, and that does not always work out.

→ **Try, "I might not understand what you're feeling right now, but your feelings are valid."**

2. "You don't need medication to be happy."

You do not know what someone has tried, what works, and what does not. What he or she might need is up to the discretion of his or her healthcare provider, mental health professionals, and himself or herself. To be frank, you do not *know* if someone needs medication or not. Medication is not a solution that works for everyone, but they are trying not to knock it before they try it.

→ **Try being supportive and understanding. Medication is not a one-size-fits-all solution, but do not make them feel even more alone by judging their decision to take medication.**

3. "Get out of bed, then maybe you'll feel better."

Without knowledge of what depression may entail or how it may affect someone, this can seem like a good thing to say.

Surely, staying in bed and ruminating with your thoughts can make you feel like you are unable to break out of the cycle of negative thinking—so why not just get out of bed? It is not always that easy to just do things that seem simple, such as getting out of bed, in a normal mindset. But when someone is depressed, this can be a real struggle. Brushing your teeth, eating, or just getting up can all be incredibly difficult to do when you are in a deep depression.

→ If you want to try to do something with your friend, then great! But do it gently. **Try: "Would you like to go out with me today? We can just go for a walk. If that's too hard, I can just keep you company."** It might help them feel better knowing you just want to spend time with them, even if they are in a sad state. Do not force them to do anything that might require too much energy.

4. "Stay busy, so you do not have time to be sad."

While this is definitely one of my tactics, you should not tell someone who is depressed to stay busy. For many people, the reality that their depression brings is the lack of motivation, the want to be alone and not "bothering" anyone.

→ **Try putting yourself in their shoes, and realize different things work for different people.** I would not tell someone to stay busy even though it is something that works for me, as it somewhat invalidates their experience, and that is one of the last things you want to do! It would be nice if you can help them figure out what might work for them, simply by being there for your loved one with depression.

It is important for us to break the stigma surrounding mental health for several reasons.

Lainey, a fellow mental health advocate, thinks it is super important because "mental illness literally kills people. We are seeing young children, and people of all ages, take their own lives because they feel hopeless and like they have nowhere to turn to. We need to talk about it, we need to get uncomfortable and face the facts."

Jessica Finney says in order to break down the stigma, you should talk about what you are going through. She says, "I am constantly talking about how counseling has changed my life as if I am talking about going to my physician/dentist/a 'traditional' medical appointment. As someone in the medical field, I can now look for signs in my patients and share my own experiences while referring them to the proper resources."

Jessica also mentions that we can all hold ourselves accountable by watching for burnout in colleagues. We need to normalize mental health care as if it is just as necessary as physical health care, because it is. She says, "Do not casually throw around terms like depressed, panic attack, OCD, suicidal, etc. And do not equate emotions with weakness."

I think that it is incredibly important for us to take it upon ourselves to be more compassionate about things we do not initially understand. Moreover, we need to really learn so that we are more sensitive to the tribulations in the lives of our loved ones.

Lessons & Takeaways:

- Hold yourself accountable by learning common symptoms and recognizing them in your loved ones when they happen.
- Talk about what is going on; it opens up a platform for you to talk about your experiences, which will allow others to do the same.
- Listen before you judge.
- You rarely ever know what someone is going through, and while actions speak louder than words, assumptions can be completely wrong.
- Try to be more understanding so that you do not say something that might be more detrimental than supportive.

Chapter 7:
Someone To Talk To

A survey released by the ADAA in January 2016 found that college-aged students feel less of the stigma around mental health than their parents did. They seem to be more willing to get help when necessary as well as help their friends in times of need.

"I do know that I can talk to someone about issues though. It's nice to know that there are people here that care and are willing to listen," Ale says.

Ale grew up in a strictly Peruvian household, but as time goes by, she and her family have adopted more American ideals. Through food, holidays, and traditions, however, Ale would say she stayed true to her culture.

Similar to many immigrant families, the preservation of one's culture is incredibly important. However, the more time you spend in a different country, the more you will eventually acclimate to the norms there.

With more time spent in the United States, Ale believes that her parents are able to recognize mental health problems easier, but they still do not completely understand them.

This case is not super uncommon either. Parents can attempt to understand as best as they can, but growing up with a different mindset often can wire our brains in ways that make it difficult to completely understand someone whose upbringing was different than our own.

In terms of access to avenues of aid, her family has been able to see and realize that there are many differences between life in Peru and life in the United States. She says when her family came to the United States, the answer would be, "No way will these [mental health problems] ever be talked about!"

Compared to her family in Peru, her parents seem to be more understanding about the use of therapy. Ale is one of my best friends, and has been around through both Jady and my experiences. With what she has learned by being a part of our support systems, she has been able to take time to talk with her mom about how these things can affect everyone—even her very own best friends.

Ale's relationship with her parents is healthy, which allows them to share some things, but Ale finds that it can be somewhat of a one-way street. She often finds herself acting as a sounding board for her mom, while she does not use her mother as one in return. And with her father, she says they do not talk about everything because he is more quiet and less open about most things.

We have often seen best friendships, or two-way streets, between our white peers and their parents, but it is not as common among our friends with immigrant parents. Sometimes, we do not believe that our parents will understand, or we get brushed off when we do decide to open up.

Jessica Finney notes, "It is even possible opening up a conversation about your own mental health will cause your parents to reflect on their own mental health. But also...I think it's important to know that it's okay if you do not talk to your parents about your mental health if you're talking to others who care about you about it. If one chose to not talk to their parents about their mental health, I would encourage them to not perpetuate that pattern and be someone people can open to about their mental health."

Which brings me to mentioning that Ale would not say that she is as close with her parents as an American perspective would encourage. She feels like people in the United States are much more willing and feel much more ready to talk about certain issues with their parents from an early age.

For some topics, there are definitely boundaries that she is unable to cross, because it would not be respectful to her parents. Certain topics would definitely be taboo, so she does not necessarily feel comfortable sharing *everything* like she has seen some of our peers whose parents were also born and raised in the United States do.

Being able to just talk about problems can help, and on the other end of that is just listening, which can also help someone. It is important to make sure that when someone is attempting to open up to you about something vulnerable, that you are present and you listen.

Moreover, Ale likes to deal with her things by herself. Although it is great to work things out independently, knowing that you have someone to potentially talk to eases some stress. Having this knowledge makes it feel less overwhelming, because if things get too hard, then you know that there are people you can lean on.

She grew up with more of a "if you have an issue, let's find where it started and deal with it" type of mindset. Solutions were important. So anytime something was bothering her, she would try to get to the bottom of it, and resolve it this way. Therefore, in her opinion, her issues were not really worth stressing over.

Having someone to talk to and having a support system is wonderful because if it is built with people who love you, they will care to listen. No matter how "small" something may seem, there is someone willing to listen.

Ale thinks that her parents see that mental health problems should be talked about, which is why they often ask, "How are things?" if she seems like she is getting too stressed out. However, a commonality in immigrant parents is that they do not see therapy or talking about their mental health problems as much of an option for themselves, even though it would be understandable to seek help.

For a long time, there has been shame surrounding therapy, so it is not out of the ordinary to believe that therapy is not an option for oneself. In fact, Wong et. al, have found self-stigma to be higher for Latinx people, and they are also the least likely to use any mental health services.

Ale believes her parents have a "children first" mindset where they feel the need to look out for their children before themselves. They want solutions, which is seen in their "we can fix it now and then see if that fixed it for *good*" kind of attitude.

Regarding her sister and mental health problems, Ale says, I have an eight-year-old little sister and as far as I can see, I do not think I see any mental health problems, but I do notice that she can keep quiet when she feels down which is scary to think about when she grows up because I do not want her to feel like she cannot go to anybody. I do not think she is old enough for me to talk about my issues but I definitely let her know that she can always talk to me about anything, even if she does not feel comfortable talking about it with her parents.

I would like to think that the shows she watches and the way she's growing up with mental health issues being more talked about will make her more willing to say something, but kids are always tricky. Shows on Disney Channel do go more in depth than they ever did when we were young though!

It is important to let our siblings know, regardless of age, that we are there for them. We will always be in their court and always be there to listen.

In terms of her own problems, Ale says that she has a tendency to keep quiet about them because she overthinks where they could be coming from or why she is feeling a certain way. She finds that she will bottle it up and sleep on it and see if she still feels the same way later. She likes to think things through by herself before she brings them up to others.

I think that this is something that is not out of the ordinary; I have often kept my problems to myself for fear that I am overreacting. But I think it is also incredibly important to discuss what is going on, because our brains can be incredibly tricky! Talking to someone can help you literally get out of your own head and feel more grounded. Plus, saying things out loud makes them seem less scary sometimes.

Ale would have this advice to share with her younger self: It's okay to talk about your issues. Don't bottle things up and then explode (because that's not healthy)! Don't be afraid to say what you're feeling when you feel it; not everything needs thinking through. If you're upset, then be upset and feel it and then you can move on; just don't bottle it up!

She has been a sounding board for both Jady and myself. While she may not always talk about what is wrong, she does realize that it is completely okay to talk about it and she knows that there are people in her life she can talk to. It is important for people to know that there are people that want to know what is going on your life.

No matter how "small" something may be, there is someone that is willing to listen.

Lessons & Takeaways:

- It is important for us all to have at least one person to talk to.
- No matter how minuscule your problems may seem to you, there is someone who is willing to listen.
- It is okay to keep to yourself, but know you do not have to!
- Talking to someone can help you get out of your own head.
- Being someone to talk to and being trustworthy is a trait that never goes out of style, so always be interested in what is going on in your loved ones' lives.

Part III:
TALK

Chapter 8:
Find Support In Your Siblings

"As siblings, we understand each other more than
if we just talked to our parents. We've kind of built
our own support system, with just our siblings."

— JADY

Trigger warning: mention of suicide attempt, self-harm

My childhood best friend Jady was born in the United States
of two Chinese immigrants and has a sister as well as a
brother.

Jady is the eldest child, her sister is in the middle, and her
brother is the youngest. Siblings often fall into certain roles.
Especially as we grow up alongside each other, these roles
become more and more evident. Jady has found herself in a
role that can be considered experimental, as she is often the
first to do things.

Birth order has a considerable effect on our sibling relationships, but despite birth order affecting our personalities, having siblings can be an absolute blessing in disguise.

In traditional families, our siblings are those that are born and grow up with us for our entire lives. In my case, my sisters and I were not that close; in fact, I often found myself fighting with my little sister and getting in trouble for always bothering my older sister. Today, I proudly say that they are two of my best friends. Our siblings can easily make up a part of our support system.

In my case and in Jady's experience, our mental health journey is not one that is gone through alone—we have our siblings.

It is important to note that today, our siblings do not have to be the ones that are necessarily born into our family. There are mixed families where an adoptive or step-sibling can easily fit into our support system.

Moreover, similar to how you can choose who is in your support system, you can choose your siblings too. Nonbiological siblings are normal and having them is completely okay. I would say that I have many siblings to whom I am not related by blood.

My older sister's best friends have been around since I was in elementary school and have always been like extra big sisters to me. In fact, I call them all *Ate*, which means big sister in Tagalog, and it feels weird when I do not say *Ate* prior to saying their name.

In the same vein, my sisters and I grew up always going on trips with my god-family. I would say they are my non-biological siblings too because they have always welcomed my sisters and me into their home, no questions asked.

Siblings, by no means, have to be biological. Our cousins can be considered our siblings too. Even if you are the only child, you can still find yourself with several siblings if you look hard enough.

Having siblings means that you are able to discuss things that your parents have said or done that may surprise you. This support system gives you a space to talk about what has been going on. Additionally, these siblings, more than our peers, can understand the standards that our parents expect us to reach.

Immigrant parents have high expectations and a desire for their children to be successful. The idea that your brain might not be completely well is unheard of. In many cultures, the idea is that we all have bad days is a fact of life; we must accept it, be strong, continue working hard, and move on. But the image of being strong can often falter and then the image is broken. Sometimes, the situation reaches a breaking point before the matter becomes clear and mental health can be spoken about.

Jady was raised with very traditional Chinese values alongside individualistic and American values. Much like her peers that are children of immigrants, Jady had a respectable relationship with her parents—talking with them but not as much as we saw some of our friends talking to their parents.

Jady's parents are incredibly hard-working; they own a very successful Chinese American restaurant in our hometown. Growing up, they often worked 75+ hours a week to support Jady and her siblings.

However, mental health in her family was rarely addressed. Problems were often acknowledged, but the idea of talking about what was going on was out of the picture. In their family, the mindset was very much, "We understand that there are hardships in life, and we go through them too. But we can handle them ourselves. And we do not go asking for help."

It is a common theme to not discuss what is bothering us among both immigrant parents and children of immigrants. It takes an incredible amount of courage and bravery to discuss what is happening. Not talking about it can have negative repercussions.

Since Jady rarely spoke about her feelings and the state of her mental health, she often bottled everything up inside. When we are not given a space to talk about our feelings, it can be confusing to navigate our emotions and we allow these feelings build up…until they explode.

> **"Whenever anyone [in the family] did try to talk about feelings, it would be very uncomfortable."**

It can be seen as a weakness if we talk about anything that is bothering us, therefore bottling it up seemed to be the easier option. This is even more the case when there can be a bit of a language barrier in the family. In translation, explanations of feelings are lost. Jady mentioned,

"And maybe what we're trying to explain in English, we don't exactly know how to translate in Chinese. And even if we use, say, Google Translate, it's not going to accurately describe what we're feeling, so I think language has been a huge barrier in our ability to talk about it, which is unfortunate."

So for a while, Jady went on without letting her parents know what was going on. At 18, she wanted to broaden her horizons and move across the country and so, she went to attend college at the University of California, Berkeley in the fall of 2016. Moving away from home and everyone that you know for the first time can be extremely difficult, especially without a support system that can be there in person.

Feelings of loneliness can make people do relatively unspeakable—in general society, due to stigma—things. Jady has always been high functioning with her depression and anxiety, always attempting to push through whatever feelings might be overwhelming her.

I have seen Jady continue to stay busy instead of succumbing to any sadness or her anxious thoughts. To anyone that does not know Jady, they would never guess that she was going through something.

Someone who is high functioning—to the outside world—will often seemingly "have it together." It is extremely easy for anyone to see someone who is high functioning and to just believe everything is okay, meanwhile the feelings on the inside rarely ever match the outward appearance.

Trigger warning: *suicide; skip forward if necessary.*

Being in a new state, on the other side of the country from friends and family made my best friend feel lost…and I was not even aware of the fact that she was feeling alone and lost. One night, I woke up to a call saying Jady was in the hospital because she had attempted to overdose on painkillers. She wanted to end it all, just as a new chapter of her life was beginning.

Jady wanted to stop feeling lost and alone. She recounts taking two handfuls of Advil and saying goodbye to friends. "I started crying but almost immediately stopped because I felt like I should not feel sorry for myself and that I had no right to cry."

She recalls the police coming to her door, and said that someone called them with a tip saying she was trying to hurt herself. She felt angry and guilty for worrying her friends. Jady was vulnerable enough to share her story below:

But I did what I usually did. I shut down emotionally and pretended I was okay, and pretended that me taking a bunch of pills was normal. I did not register it as a suicide attempt. I think that was the first time I was Baker Acted** then there was another time… [redacted]. My thought process was: no one really understands what I am going through and I never felt comfortable talking about it either because people did not really believe me, I did not want people to worry about me.

But I also liked that they seem to care, but then I felt guilty for making my friends worry, and I hated myself even more for not being able to handle it all by myself. **I just felt like a failure essentially.**

> **"People who require the use of the Baker Act have often lost the power of self-control, and they are likely to inflict harm to themselves or others. It is important that the Baker Act only be used in situations where the person has a mental illness and meets all the remaining criteria for voluntary or involuntary admission..."**

One issue that Jady dealt with in regards to her mental health is that she felt competitive. She often felt like she was either very depressed ("I would try to out-depress someone," she says) or not *that* depressed compared to some people. But today, Jady says that she wishes she could tell herself then that it's not a competition to see who is the most depressed or who has the most problems. And she also would like to tell her younger self, "There's nothing wrong with being happy, or sad."

The comparison of mental illnesses or problems in one's life to the experiences of someone else has negative effects. It can minimize your own experiences when your experiences are just as valid and just as real.

Jady and her siblings have attempted to discuss mental health with their parents. Jady, being the eldest, was the first to really open up the conversation revolving around mental health issues; her sister attempted to talk about it next, and her brother tried to talk about his anxiety too.

While it is still somewhat difficult to talk about these kinds of problems with their parents, they have found a support system among each other.

Sometimes, people do not want advice. They do not want to be told what to do to get better, not yet at least—sometimes they just really want someone to hear them. People want to know they are not alone, because mental illness can feel absolutely alienating. Jady said that sometimes people are not in the mindset to hear logical solutions—people want to know that you are simply there just to listen.

> "You know what, it's hard. It's hard and you're going to feel like this. But I will always be here for you—no matter what— no matter how things get."

Jady says that is the kind of relationship she and her siblings have. Jady and her siblings are able to talk about anything—especially when it comes to mental health. They do not want to "burden" their parents with issues that they may not fully understand. But as siblings, they understand each other more than their parents really could. "We've kind of built our own support system, with just our siblings."

Jady says while she and her siblings cope with their mental illnesses differently, she thinks it is important, at least for herself, to have a routine.

"Whether we have work or not, I find the most helpful

thing is to have a routine. So if you get up everyday—even if you don't have class that day—you get up every day, say at 8 o'clock or 10, if that is too early for you. And just get up, brush your teeth. It feels a lot better. And it is not even like I wake up and I say 'Today is going to be a great day' and try to put myself in that mentality—no. It is just taking care of yourself."

As a take away, Jady wants everyone to remember, "Our parents are humans too—they're just people. And it's not necessarily our responsibility to take care of them. And eventually, it won't be their responsibility to take care of us... but if you really love each other, let's take care of each other. Let's watch out for each other."

By creating a support system with those around us, we can find that this journey does not have to be as difficult as it is alone.

Sharing Jady's story was important to me because I know that sibling relationships are not something that everyone can take advantage of. While I understand circumstances may often be less than optimal, I think that it is possible to build a support system within a sibling relationship by always prefacing a difficult conversation as just that.

Learning how to speak our mind and how to talk about our feelings with anyone is difficult, but is so incredibly essential. If we are unable to communicate what is going on, then we cannot expect those around us, even in our support system, to understand.

Lessons & Takeaways:

- Your siblings are not necessarily always your biological siblings. You can choose them and they can choose you.
- A support system is always beneficial!
- Mental illness is not a competition. Do not discount what you have been through.
- Check in with your friends. Those that seem more withdrawn, those that have just moved, or the one that just made a life transition.
- High-functioning people with disorders can often be disguised as someone that has it all together, so do not assume anything about anyone.

Chapter 9:
Talk To The Good Voices

Sometimes, our families will not be our support system and that is absolutely okay, as long as you create a support system with people who love you. Moreover, a great relationship with your parents does not mean that everything can be openly discussed and understood. In so many immigrant families, it is not as common to discuss mental health problems.

Sherry Warner, a fierce advocate of mental health, a certified recovery specialist, certified mental health first aid instructor, and certified WRAP facilitator mentions:

> **Research shows that every individual needs at least 3 to 5 people that they can count on for love and support in their life. It is a fact that people need each other. Humans can be independent, but at the same time are also interdependent. We live in families and communities and societies where the goal is for each of our strengths and skills to be pulled together for life for all. If support cannot be found within someone's own family, it must be sought**

> **elsewhere for the health and survival of the individual.**
> **Without it we digress.**

It can be difficult to discuss mental health—and having immigrant parents makes being able to talk about certain things a little more complicated. There is the want to be open about experiences but there is also a part of you that does not want to stress out your parents.

For my dearest college best friend, her experience is just this; she grew up very in tune with her Serbian, Bosnian, and Croatian roots. She told me that she never really felt as if much was American about her life—besides going to school.

"Home was a totally different world," she said. This did not allow conversations to be had regarding issues or anxieties that she had. To her, it felt like any problem she had regarding school or otherwise could not be brought into her home.

In her family, she said mental health problems are not handled or discussed. If some mental health problem comes up regarding a celebrity or someone they may know, Ena says her family reacts with a "God forbid," followed by a slow shaking of the head, and a quick change of subject.

Sometimes there is a strained relationship between children and their parents—regardless of whether or not there might be a slight cultural difference. However, for Ena, her relationship with her parents is a very good one.

"I am more grateful for them than anything else in my life, and I am so lucky to have them and to have the life I have because of them," Ena says.

Moreover, a good relationship does not mean that it is void of its faults. When asked if she is able to talk about anything with them or if there are any topics that are taboo, Ena shared this:

"That being said, I do not talk to them about anything really. I would not say that it is necessarily that things are taboo, but rather it is terrifying to talk to them about things because of their reaction to said things.

Recently I had, not quite a panic attack, but a really bad day. I was incredibly anxious and could not get anything done; all I wanted was to lie down and cry. I could not do that, so I went to the bathroom and cried. It could not have been more than five minutes when my mom came knocking on the door. I wiped my eyes and opened the door and she looked as if I had narrowly escaped a car crash. She was so worried and she frantically asked what was the matter with me. I simply said I was just feeling anxious and wanted to cry a little to release some tension. She was so worried and for the next two days asked me once an hour on the hour if I was okay.

I hated it and it pained me to see her so worried, and it was not helping my anxiety to be asked every hour if I was okay. The way she would ask felt like I was on the brink of doing something awful. I wanted to scream that this was just my standard anxiety—that I have felt so much worse so she should not be worried. But I was terrified I would be committed somewhere. My dad is not even an option really to talk about my anxiety, he just gets mad about it…I cannot handle that."

Additionally, in Ena's family, therapy is seen as "a solution for broken people." However, therapy is usually not frowned upon if someone else was doing it—it is understood that they are doing something helpful and good for their own well-being.

On the other hand, if Ena ever mentioned therapy as an option for herself, her parents would be worried and she would be asked, "Why? What's wrong with you?" Ena says that nothing has to be "wrong" with her, and she is not broken. She is just a human that feels things and wants an outlet to discuss those feelings.

Jessica Finney, University of Florida Doctor of Physical Therapy student, says that we should talk to our friends, siblings, and trusted adults such as teachers or professors, professional mentors, and parents of friends. Or if possible, talk to a licensed mental health counselor or your physician. Gather your thoughts together by talking to people you trust.

Since therapy is still stigmatized in Ena's family, she deals with her problems by listening to her favorite podcast—My Favorite Murder. She said that discovering it helped her feel not only entertained and distracted, but also not alone. She relates to the hosts and feels comfortable when listening to it, and she said that the hosts have changed her so much.

Ena also copes by talking to someone, as speaking her anxieties aloud helps her to step away and hear that the anxieties sound silly, which allows them to instantly fade away.

"That is why you should not listen to the mean voices in your head, they want you to feel anxious. Talk to the good voices in your life instead, and it'll help you to clear your head and get all the weight off your chest."

Additionally, one of the hosts from Ena's favorite podcast, Georgia Hardstark, talks about how you have to be kind to the "little you." You would never be mean or awful to your younger self, and so whenever you talk to yourself or think about yourself, pretend as if you are talking to your little self.

> **Would you say the awful things you say about yourself to the little you? Of course not. So, I would tell my younger self the things that I try to tell myself now—that life can be awful and mean, and that you may never be totally happy with yourself. But that's okay—because sometimes life is so beautiful and things work out so wonderfully, and that you are going to do things you never even imagined. Also that no matter how you feel, you really are not alone. Do not listen to all the mean voices in your head. Listen to your best friend since 2nd grade's voice. Or listen to the voice of the friend who helped you transition into college and adulthood. Listen to the voice of the person who loves you when you did not think it was possible for someone to love you because those voices are not biased. They do not have an agenda, the mean voices in your head do. Do not trust them.**

The good voices are the voices of those who love you, those that care about you and are there for you when things get difficult. Although it can be hard to not listen to the mean voices, always listen to the good voices.

Talking about what is happening in your life and all of the little anxieties can make someone more anxious because they can start thinking about all of the ways that someone might react. Talking about it is important though because no one is a mind reader (*unless you actually can read minds, but that is a whole different conversation that might need to be had*).

To children who find it difficult to talk about mental health with their parents, Sherry Warner says:

> **My best advice and thoughts to a child who is struggling to discuss mental health with their parents is to find a way to connect and build a relationship that respects and honors the worldview of the person they are trying to open up to and to be armed with as much research on the topic as possible. Instead of approaching the topic from a point of view that assumes and fosters a gap, foster an approach that starts with an attitude of mutuality- 'we are in this together,' 'let's learn about this together,' 'we both want the same thing- health and happiness for our family.' Starting with the relationship first and a shared goal to keep that relationship healthy and strong can make all the difference. Be mindful however, that in some instances, after all you can do, all you can say, and all you bring to the table, that we can not force**

> **another person to think about life as we do. Sometimes distance is necessary for health. Those times are unfortunate, but must be considered if a relationship is toxic.**

As a parent of five, she says that parents can help in discussions with their children regarding mental health by being open-minded and learning all that they can in order to understand the information that is available regarding mental health. They can also help by being introspective and trying to understand their own biases, worldviews, and reasons for how they think, speak, and do. Self-reflection and space for another person's thoughts and feelings can bring greater connection to those relationships.

Unfortunately, if we do not start discussing and opening the conversation up about our experiences, people will never know what you are going through. Talking about our own experiences is important in letting people know that they are not alone. The chances of you knowing someone (or knowing someone who knows someone) with a mental health condition is very high. It is more common than you think.

Normalizing mental health issues can be difficult, and is difficult to navigate with anxiety, but knowing that there are good voices in your life can help you feel less alone. Knowing that you can talk about your experiences with a select group of people is vital.

It is important to find solace in the support system that you are able to make.

Lessons & Takeaways:

- Every individual needs about three to five people whom they can lean on for love and support.
- A good relationship is not void of faults.
- When your brain might be saying bad things, remember the good voices—the voices of those who love you—instead.
- Therapy is not a solution for broken people, it is useful for anyone.
- If we do not talk about things going on with us, no one will ever really know.

Chapter 10:
Share Your Story

———

As a mental health professional and licensed clinical social worker, Alexis Pardo says, "I think sharing our own stories is helpful. Everyone thinks other people have it together, but not them. The truth is that everyone is struggling with their own issues."

For children that find it difficult to discuss mental health with their parents, Alexis believes that two things typically need to happen: setting healthy boundaries and sharing how **you** can be best supported during difficult periods of your life. She also says that alternatively, at the end of the day, we have to be with okay with possibly not understanding what we are going through. "You can clearly communicate your needs, but if the receiver is not willing to receive the message, then what is plan B?" she says.

She recommends remembering your values as well as self-care. Moreover, she thinks that we can help our peers by normalizing mental health and increasing awareness of the issue. Simply talking about it and allowing the conversation can provide a space for someone to discuss their experiences.

While it is important for us to talk about it, it is also important for people to realize that they should provide a listening ear—if needed. She says that listening is one of the most valuable tools we all possess. We do not need to have all the answers or solve any problems; sometimes just being there and holding space for someone is the most therapeutic thing we can do for them. We do not need to have gone through the same thing or even something similar to recognize when someone is hurting.

Jessica Finney had this to add on finding a way to share your story: "Write down your thoughts so you can see it on paper. Write what you would say to your parents if you could say anything and not feel judged. What's worse: keeping your experience a secret or the potential for rejection or misunderstanding? It's not a rhetorical question, I think it's the choice the person has to make when choosing whether or not to broach the topic and how deep they want to go into the topic."

Simply putting yourself in another person's position and treating them how you think they would want to be treated is important. If someone trusts you enough to confide in you, chances are you know them well enough to gauge whether or not they want someone to listen or are actually seeking a solution.

Alexis offers one possible response: "I cannot even imagine what it is like to go through that, but I can see that this hurts you." Try that, instead of saying anything that begins with, "Well on the bright side…"

Parents can help by asking directly asking, "How can I help you through this?" She says this alone is powerful, and we do not need to understand why something is the way that it is. If it is affecting someone we love, we figure out how to help because it matters to that person. Additionally, asking if someone wants to simply vent or if they want a solution can be beneficial for both parties. Asking a direct question will most likely lead to a direct answer.

Jessica adds, "It could also be helpful to attempt to educate parents prior to discussion. 'I learned this interesting thing at school…' This would allow you to get a read of the room before continuing the conversation."

Alexis wants to reiterate that we can change the perception of mental health and the stigma enveloping it by sharing our own personal stories and experiences with mental health. She also adds, "Everyone has moments when things feel like they are falling apart. Sharing with others about our struggles and our resources that helped us makes everyone feel less alone. Talking to our friends, coworkers, family members, and our loved ones helps to break down the stigma that surrounds mental health."

Moreover, not everyone has a support system, but with the age that we live in today, there are so many resources that we can find online and through social media. However, we can also find these through our local communities, Alexis advises.

And for ease, at the end of this book, I have compiled a list of several resources that I have found are available or affordable online.

Plus, if therapy is not as accessible for some, she thinks that books, workbooks, and even YouTube videos are helpful. She tends to recommend books written by Brené Brown, Tara Brach, Steven Hayes, and Pema Chodron.

Additionally, if you find that you are alone in your journey, Alexis says that mindfulness and gratefulness are two of the most important skills that anyone can learn. Mindfulness can be practiced by tuning into your senses, practicing deep breathing, and pausing, while gratefulness can be practiced through journaling in a daily gratitude journal.

Anyone can break the stigma, but in order to do this, we must keep the conversation going and share our stories. Plus, Alexis cannot stress enough how important it is that we practice our right to vote. She says, "Believe in your political efficacy. Making mental health services available to more people starts at the policy level."

She says that we all have a personal responsibility to find ways to advocate and educate ourselves. There are many opportunities out there to help, especially if we look for them.

Moreover, to people trying to break down the stigma, Sherry Warner says:

Do not get discouraged if at first people do not understand your goals in trying to break down stigma. The only way we make change in this life is be speaking up and getting involved. Our silence is a message in and of itself. It means we are ok with the way things are. If we aren't, and our conscience urges us to speak up and we can do so loudly and with kindness, we can find ourselves in a position to be a powerful agent for change.

Regarding breaking the stigma, Christina Pfister University of North Florida Nursing Student, had this to add:

It is extremely important to break down the stigma for mental health. What most do not understand is that your mental health is just as important as your physical health. When you have an infection or diabetes you go to the doctor to fix it and to be treated for it. Mental health is the exact same thing, but most people see it as lesser than because sometimes there is no outward cause or symptom and that's part of where the stigma lies. It can be written off easier and go untreated. We have inadvertently been trained as a society to see mental health issues as lesser than, when in reality it is just as important as going to get antibiotics when you have strep throat. The stigma needs to be broken so that going to therapy or even going to an inpatient facility are on the same level of importance as going to the hospital for something else. Treatment for mental illness should not be an afterthought anymore and breaking this stigma will allow people to start to not only feel more comfortable in seeking help but also speaking out about their struggles.

Wish I Could Tell My Parents...

If we step off the paths that are already paved, we can make a change. And change does not happen if we fall into a routine of being afraid to speak out. We need to use the platforms and voices that are given to us.

Talking about mental health and communicating with those close to you is important. Even if you find that it is difficult, attempt to find the strength within yourself to talk about what is going on in your mind.

In her experience, Jessica recounted that something that her parents specifically did to support her mental health journey was simply understanding that some of her anxieties and problems were rooted in things they had done. "They had not done any of these things on purpose to harm me. I understand they were trying their best. Telling them specifically what happened and how I needed to reshape our boundaries was scary. I was worried they would be defensive and recoil against me. I was worried I would hurt their feelings. I am grateful for their grace in accepting the information and helping me in the best way they knew how moving forward from that time."

We need to talk about it with our family and our friends— and we also need to listen to those who are brave enough to share their stories with us.

I still wish I could tell my mother that my mental health matters more than money. I would rather spend thousands of dollars trying to get better and get help, instead of ignoring my problems and just hoping and praying that it will go away. No, I would not go to a doctor every week, but my mental health problems are so different from any treatable physical problem. Sometimes I wish I could die, and my therapist helps me face my problems head-on. I think that in the long run, my appointments are worth the investment. I wish you felt like my well-being is worth all the money in the world. I love you, but please understand that this is a better outcome than what my brain wishes sometimes.

Sigiana wishes she could tell her parents: "Mental health does not care about circumstance, it is not something that only comes for you in your worst of times but instead it's something that can make a perfect day feel like a nightmare. I wish they could understand that my mental health does not reflect their parenting and that my mental health does not make me a weak person. Most of all I wish I could tell them that mental health is something that needs to be taken seriously and needs to be addressed."

Ale wishes she could tell her parents: "It is okay to take time for yourselves to talk about mental health honestly with yourself first and then with someone else. Just because you never thought about it as a possibility in your life ever doesn't mean that you can never talk about what you have gone through." She feels like there are some things in their past that they still dwell on and that should be talked through whether together or apart.

Jady wishes she could tell her parents: "Everybody's experience of life, what stresses them out, and what can be too much to handle is very different. It's okay for you to be completely stressed out, and it's okay to talk about what's going on instead of trying to act tough. In the end, the only person you're hurting whenever you try to act tough is yourself. And I just think, if I could tell them in their own language, I think it'd be more impactful for them to hear it in Chinese rather than in English for me to say, 'Hey, it's okay for you to be sad. It's okay for you to have down days. I know you're my parents, but you don't have to be strong all the time."

"It's not you that makes me feel the way that I do. I love you with everything that I can." —Angi

"I wish I could tell my dad that forcing religion on me and telling me that my mental illness wasn't real wouldn't help my mental health!"- Friend who would like to remain anonymous

"My progress isn't linear, some days are bad, some days are good! Please be patient with me." —Alex

"I do care and love you. It's just that I don't like it when you don't give me enough support."

"Intergenerational trauma is real...and it needs to [be] dealt with." -Ash

"I just want stability and I know you're trying your best."

Lastly, Ena wishes she could tell her parents that everyone experiences mental health problems to some extent. She wants them to know that she is not rare, or "broken" for having anxiety. Also, she wishes they knew that while she has serious issues with anxiety that sometimes can be debilitating, she is not wrong or broken for it, and it's normal to have these feelings sometimes. She wishes that they would not constantly worry or think about her since it only exacerbates her anxiety—and she wishes it could be normalized a little more because "taking care of my mental health and talking about my mental health is just as important as talking about my stomachaches or headaches and they should not freak out."

I found that it was important to share some things from my friends about what they wish they could tell their parents. It is difficult to share your story with people that may seem like they do not care.

I believe it is important for us to just write it out, to say something out loud to someone that you love. I know that it is scary to be vulnerable and nerve-wracking to put yourself out there and give yourself a platform to talk, but it is so vital for us to do so.

Everyone has a story to share. I have asked only a few of my friends to share their stories, or simply things that they wish they could tell their parents, with me.

Imagine if you asked your friends what they wish they could say. Imagine what you would learn from asking such a simple question.

Lessons & Takeaways:

- Everyone thinks other people have it together, but not them. The truth is that everyone is struggling with their own issues.
- Anyone can break the stigma, but in order to do this, we must keep the conversation going and share our stories.
- Listening to stories is just as important as sharing them.
- Parents can help by simply asking, "How can I help you?"
- Think of the Platinum Rule: Treat people the way you think they want to be treated. (Not the Golden Rule—Do not treat them the way you want to be treated, because the way you want to be treated may not be the way they want to be treated.)

Part IV:
IMPROVE

Chapter 11:
Learning To Ask For Help

―――――――

Trigger warning: mention of self-harm

Under the umbrella that is psychotherapy, Cognitive Behavior Therapy is a treatment that helps clients understand the relationship between thoughts and feelings—and thus how behaviors are affected by their thoughts and feelings. We can only control our behaviors and our thoughts—not so much how we feel.

Cognitive Behavior Therapy helps us to challenge our thoughts and what we are going to do about things that may affect us. Mental illness has affected several of my loved ones—but the difference can be as simple as asking, what steps can you take to better yourself? Learning to ask for help when you are not getting the help that you need is one of the biggest steps that can be taken.

Another one of my childhood best friends, Jane, was the first to be born in the United States out of her immediate family. Growing up, she had a more Americanized experience than her older sisters, while simultaneously being influenced heavily by Filipino culture. She said that growing up with her mixed cultures involved a lot of social pressure to fit in at school while also dealing with the economic struggle that many immigrant families run into.

Jane's relationship with her parents has always been typical—she talked to them often, got along with them, and argued with them. But until middle school, she did not realize how strained her relationship with her parents was. Middle school can be exciting, but it comes with other realizations. For Jane, it was the first time she was ever allowed to spend the day at a friend's house, where she began to notice our peers' relationships with their parents.

Our friends seemed to have more involved parents—Jane recalls that their parents would often join in on conversations regarding other people in classes, drama with friends and teachers, and even comment on popular trends among kids our age. She recalls that our friends' parents seemed to be aware, and that she never spoke to her parents like our friends spoke to theirs—like a friend. Her family does not discuss relationships, personal drama, and most notably, mental health.

This was also the first time she felt like she did not want to be alive anymore. In her family, depression is a careless and ugly word. Depression and suicide are taboo words—they are words that exemplify the failure of her parents. In middle school, her mental health came into question for the first time, which was very foreign ground for everyone involved.

Jane is an incredibly talented and beautiful storyteller. Below she recounts her experiences with mental health.

There was me, too afraid to cry in front of my family; there were my parents, too scared to know whether it [was] serious or a phase; and there were the school counselors, unsure how to navigate a situation where their morality told them to protect the child and tell the parents, while also telling them that the child had some truth in her voice when she spoke of her fear of her parents finding out.

I purposely hurt myself for the first time in middle school. Even now, trying to relive those first few times hurts somewhere deep inside. Whether it be a repressed memory or general forgetting, I do not even think I can really remember much of the aftermath of that time in my life. I remember feeling scared, not for my own safety anymore, but for the consequences that my parents would surely bring on me. I remember feeling helpless as my sisters got involved and cried on the phone to me in a mix of anger and sadness. It was like everyone around me was both furious with my actions and sad about my state of being. And as quickly as it started, it was gone, swept under the rug and tucked away like a stain being covered by mother's brand new rug.

College was the second round of my struggles with my mental health, and it felt as if something out there was seeking revenge on me for brushing it off the first time. This second bout of depression landed me in both therapy and psychiatry for about 8 months. Various concoctions of Celexa,

Zoloft, Welbutrin, and other SSRIs and antidepressants eventually brought me back to stability. My parents, still to this day, do not know that it ever got as bad as it did, but they did see that things were different from middle school, they saw a real change in my attitude. Going into the specifics of what happened to me in college seems unproductive and spiteful of those involved, but it was arguably one of the hardest times in my life. I had not left my bed except for the bathroom and for my daily half-meal of soup and rice for three months between September and November of 2018, and in retrospect, this is probably where my parents started to feel a real genuine concern for my wellbeing. At the end of it all, I have come to stop blaming people, I have come to stop harboring so much anger towards my parents and what I assumed to be their ignorance towards my situation. In fact, I feel lucky to have even warranted some of the empathy they showed me in college after seeing the lack of it that my sisters received when they experienced their own struggles.

To Mom and Dad, I wish you could have seen how hard all of this has been for me, I wish you could have felt the things I felt in all this time, but I am also thankful that you did not. I am thankful you and my sisters never had to know what this felt like. I wish you could see that it wasn't just time or personal motivation that got me to where I am now, it was a mix of those things with professional medical help.

After struggling with what would make my family happy and what would make me happy, I made the decision to seek help and actually go to therapy. I started seeing Vincent, my therapist for the next year. It was hard for me to find the words to express what was happening, especially to a complete stranger who had no way of understanding what my family background was. If I could not even talk to my own siblings, people who had watched me grow up my entire life, how could I talk to this 40-year-old man who did not even know the first thing about me? It took me several months to realize that my hesitation in talking to Vincent was not because of distrust, it was because I felt that I could not convince him to understand what was happening to me and to truly believe how all of it was affecting me.

Eventually, I realized that the only way I was going to be able to really accept any of his help and advice was to stop treating him like a doctor and to see him as a friend. Once that barrier started to come down, the conversations flowed more naturally, I felt myself look forward to our weekly sessions. Perhaps one of the most ironically comforting moments in my time with Vincent was when he admitted to me that he, alone, could not help me. From there, I met Dr. Chen, a sweet Asian-American psychiatrist who not only related to me in terms of family dynamics, but also with age. Dr. Chen was relatively young, younger than most of the other psychiatrists that were available. Vincent and Dr. Chen met regularly to discuss my progress and my condition, and their collaboration and commitment to my wellbeing eventually brought me to where I am today.

The past year was—of course—not a straightforward incline to happiness. There were periods where I skipped my session, days where I felt that Vincent and Dr. Chen were not listening or did not understand. But I trusted that they knew what they were doing, I reminded myself that they were human just like me and could have bad days just like anyone else.

It was breaking the stigma of mental health in an immigrant Asian-American family and being diagnosed with a high-functioning anxiety and bipolar disorder, and learning to ask for help and treatment when I needed it.

Being able to simply take back control from your mental illness is difficult. Jane decided to take control back, say, "I am not my mental illness," and come out stronger than ever. Being able to ask for help is one of the most difficult things, and I am so proud of her. We do not realize what our closest friends go through sometimes and sometimes you get a phone call—asking for any advice, asking for just someone to help them feel like they are not "crazy" for feeling this way.

When I got a call from Jane in the fall of 2018, she was lost and I did not know how to help. Sometimes I do not, because I am not a professional. I slightly remember mentioning that therapy has helped me and having my two cats as emotional support animals helps me get out of bed.

I gave her the only knowledge I had—but she took things into her very own hands and sought the help she needed. It is incredibly important to get out of our heads and do something when it seems like things are getting to be too much.

Lessons & Takeaways:

- Despite what those around you might think, you need to do what is best for you and your health.
- Only you are able to take the steps needed to better yourself.
- It is unproductive to blame anyone for what you are going through.
- Viewing a mental health professional as just their credentials may not help much; it takes a bit of rewiring to accept that they simply just want to help you get better.
- Getting help is not a one-way ticket to happy town. Healing is a long road.

Chapter 12:
One Size Does Not Fit All

———

Regardless of whether you have one immigrant parent or two, mental health can still be stigmatized. It is important to remember how stigmatized it still is in non-immigrant families. Mental health does not discriminate and therefore there is not one solution that works for everyone.

Not only is mental health important to talk about, but it is also equally important to get help. There are several ways of coping with mental health problems—whether it be in the form of a support system, being able to speak about it openly or being able to talk about it in therapy. Sometimes, seeking help means getting medication to make things more bearable. There are so many solutions that are available, and what works for you might not work for the next person.

In Nicole's experience, only one of her parents is an immigrant. However, that does not bar her from experiencing any mental health problems, nor does it prevent her mother from being diagnosed with a mental health problem.

Nicole grew up in a very Americanized culture with very little influence from her mother's Indian and Malay side. Unfortunately, she never learned how to speak Malay and found it difficult to communicate with her grandmother.

When a parent decides to assimilate into a new culture, sometimes this ability to speak a different language is not practiced, and therefore lost. In my family, while my sisters and I can understand the language, similar to Nicole, we cannot speak it.

The life that many immigrants always strive for is the American Dream. Nicole's mother had dreamed of coming to the United States and wanted to achieve the "American Dream" with 2.5 kids and a white-picket fence. When she was 25 years old, she finally got the opportunity to come to the United States and pursue this.

Fast forward a bit, Nicole and her older brother were born, and so when they started growing up, her mother often labeled herself as a Tiger Mom—meaning she identified her parenting style not as authoritarian but as one that enforced strict rules, had tough love, and had high expectations for her children. Not only did she want the best for her children, she pushed her husband to do his best too, and told him to return to school in order to get a better job.

For many Asian families, Tiger parents are often our reality. This in addition to our own standards can make things slightly difficult at times, especially as a child when you generally do what you are told.

Nicole's mom was a Registered Nurse up until she was in middle school, and unfortunately, she lost her job due to workplace discrimination. Around this time, things were not necessarily ideal, and this was around the same time that Nicole's mom told both her and her brother that she had been diagnosed with Depression.

At 13, Nicole did not know much about mental health issues nor did she understand how her mom would smile sometimes if she were depressed—she did not understand how this affected her mother or what it really meant. Her mom simply told her and her brother that she had depression and the conversation did not continue.

I have found that my mother has behaved similarly; several important things are said but once, and then never discussed again.

When Nicole was younger, she had a great relationship with both her mom and her dad. But being the Tiger Mom she was, her mother began slowly pushing Nicole away, to push her to do good things in her own life. And even though Nicole was closer to her father, she never mentioned any of her problems or struggles with him because she wanted to be seen as a perfect daughter. *cue Reflections from Mulan* So this left her in a place where she did not feel comfortable talking to either of her parents about anything potentially vulnerable.

The risk of having a mental illness if one of your parents has one is much stronger if they have an anxiety disorder,

ADHD, alcoholism or drug abuse, bipolar disorder, depression, or schizophrenia. With this in mind, just because one parent might have a diagnosis does not mean that you will also be diagnosed with a mental health condition. But on the flip side, it does not mean that if your parents are not diagnosed, that you cannot have a mental health condition.

There is not one influence—genetic, environmental, or situational—that is stronger than another. Each influence has an equal chance to be the reason why a "flip" so to speak, is switched. This is why education, prevention, treatment, and advocacy are all important tools in combating mental health problems.

High school is often not as dreamy as it is in movies and this age can often be the onset for many mental health issues— teenage years and early 20s are often when we see the onset of several mental illnesses— but this knowledge does not mean that it will be life-altering. A diagnosis is not a death sentence, nor does it define you.

Once Nicole got to high school, her mom started making efforts to really distance herself from Nicole and began to push her really strongly towards getting good grades, getting a boyfriend, and participating in several extracurriculars.

In attempts to position their children for greatness and success, immigrant parents can often strain their relationships with their children by putting expectations on them. Sometimes, children really just want love and support—in addition to satisfying their parents' expectations.

Her sophomore year, Nicole started struggling with mental illness. She recalls sitting in her bed for hours and just staring at the wall; she never let her mother come into the room, so her mom did not know what she was going through.

However, she remembers that her mom used to let her take "Mental Health Days" in high school; her mom would call the school to let them know that she was feeling under the weather and she would rest all day. She recalls doing this with her mom when she was overwhelmed by school and stressed out by projects. However, her mom never actually asked if she was okay or asked how she was doing. Moreover, Nicole never felt that the "Mental Health Days" provided any catharsis considering she would just sit and watch mindless television shows for hours.

Sometimes this kind of unproductive Mental Health Day can be more detrimental because the root of the problem is not discovered, therefore no catharsis can be reached.

In terms of therapy, as a family, they went for a while when their home was foreclosed. The late 2000s and the economic recession hit many people hard. Nicole's family started going to counseling as a family unit, and her parents separated for a few months—but Nicole never spoke a single word to her therapist. She wanted her parents to be together again, *not* to talk about her feelings regarding anything.

In regards of seeking therapy for her mental health conditions, it was not necessarily frowned upon, but it often was not seen as a viable option by her parents.

Considering their mother told her and her brother about her diagnosis of Depression, Nicole understands that Anxiety is often the other side of the same coin. While she cannot speak on her brother's part regarding his mental health, she can guess that he has some concerns of his own.

She recalls that since they were little, he would wait by the window for their parents to come home, just worrying and imagining all of the bad things that could potentially happen to them. Never did Nicole think that a word could be assigned to those thoughts until she learned that those thoughts stem from Anxiety.

Other than her partner, her brother was the only person that she would confide in regarding her health problems for a few weeks, because she did not feel comfortable talking about her state of well-being. Now, she says, her brother is one of her best friends—a sibling that has been through nearly the same experiences. In their family, they have been through so much together. She adds that they always stand up for one another and support each other in everything one hundred percent.

Nicole did not do anything to take care of her mental health until she turned 21. She recalls months of chest pains and anxiety attacks. "Anxiety can manifest in several ways and one form that is can come in is chest pains," she says. Nicole says she was triaged after not doing anything about it at the Counseling and Wellness Center at the University of Florida. Her provider gave her a referral for a psychiatrist and she has been on medication ever since.

While in school, she was on a higher dose of Lexapro than she is now. There are so many types of anxiety medications and one size does not fit all. Working together, Nicole and her psychiatrist decided on trying Lexapro because it had worked for her mom for her depression, and now it works for Nicole's anxiety. *As previously stated, many medications treat both sides of the same coin.*

Anxiety is an individual experience and she prefers to be alone through it because she mostly goes through by herself. So Nicole finds that when she feels overwhelmed, it can be cathartic to just walk. With her headphones in, she takes long walks and has found this is what works for her.

She wishes her parents would understand that choosing to be on medication does not make her weak. Anxiety is debilitating and Nicole wishes they could understand and feel how hard it is some days. Moreover, she wishes she could tell her younger self:

"Not everyone thinks the same way as you do. Not everyone gets that stomach-dropping feeling. There's nothing wrong with you—but there is something or someone that could help. And there are so many other people that are going through similar things, but they are just afraid to talk about it too."

Additionally, Nicole mentioned that she thought that for 21 years of her life, everyone felt the feelings that she had—but now realizes that it was her anxiety.

Taking control back from Anxiety can be difficult, especially if you do not know what the culprit is, how it manifests, and how it can affect you. Nicole did something about these feelings and decided to get medication for herself. Medication is not a weakness, and it does not make anyone a weak person for deciding to take medication. In actuality, it takes strength to ask for help and medicine to make a mental health condition more bearable.

Lessons & Takeaways:

- Mental health does not discriminate and therefore there is not one solution that works for everyone.
- Not everyone thinks the same way that you do, so talking about things that bother you is completely okay.
- Parents, while you want the best for your children, always remember that your love and support should always be at the forefront.
- Again, your siblings can be some of your biggest supporters in your journey.
- Medication takes some trial and error as well, so be patient, and find what works for you.

Resources

As stated previously, I am not a professional, so my advice should be taken as mere suggestions.

Mental Health Wellness is a long road and there is not one thing that works for every single person.

Although we live in a time where many resources are very accessible, I figured it would be appropriate to include a chapter of some resources that I have found useful.

Jessica Finney adds, "If the person is in school, many schools offer free counseling. Finding a healthy activity that can reliably make you feel calm and safe is great (mine is watching John Mulaney comedy specials in bed). Doing something productive, no matter how small will help. Exercise and eating healthy when possible are helpful."

She recommended **the National Alliance on Mental Illness**. Their website can help you find a lot of local chapters, which could be a good educational resource: nami.org.

From NAMI's Website, they offer the top HelpLine Resources:

- **Anxiety and Depression Association of America (ADAA)** provides information on prevention, treatment and symptoms of anxiety, depression and related conditions.

Website: https://adaa.org/

Telephone: (240-485-1001)

- **Children and Adults with Attention-Deficit/Hyperactivity Disorder (CHADD)** provides information and referrals on ADHD, including local support groups.

  Website: http://www.chadd.org/

  Telephone: (800-233-4050)

- **Depression and Bipolar Support Alliance (DBSA)** provides information on bipolar disorder and depression, offers in-person and online support groups and forums.

  Website: https://www.dbsalliance.org/

  Telephone: (800-826-3632)

- **International OCD Foundation** provides information on OCD and treatment referrals.

  Website: https://iocdf.org

  Telephone: (617-973-5801)

- **National Center of Excellence for Eating Disorders (NCEED)** provides up-to-date, reliable and evidence-based information about eating disorders.

  Website:https://www.nceedus.org/

  Telephone: (800-931-2237)

- **Schizophrenia and Related Disorders Alliance of America (SARDAA)** offers Schizophrenia Anonymous self-help groups and toll-free teleconferences.

  Website: http://www.sardaa.org/

Telephone: (240-423-9432)

- **Sidran Institute** helps people understand, manage and treat trauma and dissociation; maintains a helpline for information and referrals.

  Website: http://www.sidran.org/

  Telephone: (410-825-8888)

- **Treatment and Research Advancements for Borderline Personality Disorder (TARA)** offers a referral center for information, support, education and treatment options for BPD.

  Website: http://www.tara4bpd.org/

  Telephone: (888-482-7227)

Suicide And Crisis

- **The Crisis Textline**: Simply text HELLO to 741741 if you're in the United States to get connected to a Crisis Counselor via text message.
- **National Suicide Prevention Lifeline:** If you are in crisis and want someone to talk to immediately, please call 1-800-273-TALK (8255)
- **The American Foundation for Suicide Prevention:** Has resources on loss and suicide prevention information. Website: https://afsp.org (888-333-2377)
- **The National Domestic Violence Hotline:** Provides 24/7 crisis intervention, safety planning and information on domestic violence.
  Website: http://www.thehotline.org/
  Telephone: (800-799-7233)

Treatment

- **Psychology Today:** A national directory of therapists, psychiatrists, therapy groups and treatment facility options.
  Website: https://psychologytoday.com
- **Open Path Collective:** A collection of therapists that offer their services at a cheaper rate.
  Website: https://openpathcollective.org
- **Recovery Inc:** Online and in-person group therapy.
  Website: https://recoveryinternational.org/
- **Better Help:** Online therapy option and cheaper than traditional therapy. Will work with you if you have money issues.
  Website: https://www.betterhelp.com/
- **Samaritans:** Email a trained counselor anonymously.
  Website: https://www.samaritans.org/
- **Mindspot:** Free eight-week courses in dealing with depression and anxiety.
  Website: https://mindspot.org.au
- **Mood Gym:** Online self-help workbook for anxiety and depression. Effective and low priced.
  Website: https://moodgym.com.au/

Final Note From Author

I do hope I instilled a new hope into you. The future of mental health is dependent on whether or not we take matters into our own hands and be better. Our voices matter. Even if you think no one is listening, if you can inspire one person, then they will inspire one more person. It is a ripple effect.

Our voices have so much power. We should do good with our voices. Be the change and be the good in the world.

My work here is not finished. I will never stop trying to break the stigma, but I do hope that you join me in this fight. We are stronger together. We never have to do anything alone.

I genuinely mean it when I say I try my hardest to be a listening ear for anyone that might need to talk about whatever you are going through. Even if I am struggling, I will never hesitate to ensure that you do not feel alone.

I hope you find peace and happiness.Be a light in the world and never let anyone turn it off.

Works Cited

1. Albano, Anne Marie. "Ending Mental Health Stigma for Generations to Come." Anxiety and Depression Association of America, ADAA. Accessed June 17, 2019. https://adaa.org/learn-from-us/from-the-experts/blog-posts/ending-mental-health-stigma-generations-come.

2. "A new plan for anxious feelings: escape the custard! | Neil Hughes | TEDxLeamingtonSpa" YouTube video. 14:14. "TEDx Talks." March 29, 2016. https://www.youtube.com/watch?v=bM06o26PCDQ.

3. "Baker Act." UF Health, University of Florida Health. April 22, 2019. Accessed July 07, 2019. https://ufhealth.org/baker-act.

4. Byrne, Peter. "Stigma of Mental Illness and Ways of Diminishing It." *Advances in Psychiatric Treatment* 6, no. 1 (January 2000): 65-72. Accessed May 10, 2019. doi:10.1192/apt.6.1.65.

5. Digital image. https://www.nimh.nih.gov/health/statistics/images/personality-comorbidity-table_155492_1.jpg.

6. "Generalized Anxiety Disorder (GAD)." Anxiety and Depression Association of America, ADAA. Accessed

July 07, 2019. https://adaa.org/understanding-anxiety/
generalized-anxiety-disorder-gad.

7. "Great Expectations: Exploring Family Dynamics and
Stress Among Asian-Americans/Pacific Islanders."
American Psychological Association. Accessed July 07,
2019. https://www.apa.org/pi/oema/resources/ethnici-
ty-health/asian-american/.

8. Harvard Health Publishing. "Understanding the Stress
Response." Harvard Health. Accessed April 21, 2019.
https://www.health.harvard.edu/staying-healthy/under-
standing-the-stress-response.

9. Loya, Fred, Radhika Reddy, and Stephen P. Hinshaw.
"Mental Illness Stigma as a Mediator of Differences in
Caucasian and South Asian College Students Attitudes
toward Psychological Counseling." *Journal of Counseling
Psychology* 57, no. 4 (October 2010): 484-90. doi:10.1037/
a0021113.

10. Mayo Clinic Staff. "Mental Health: Overcoming the
Stigma of Mental Illness." Mayo Clinic. May 24, 2017.
Accessed July 06, 2019. https://www.mayoclinic.org/
diseases-conditions/mental-illness/in-depth/men-
tal-health/art-20046477.

11. Mental Health, and Adaa. "College-Aged Adults Face
Less Mental Health Stigma." Anxiety and Depression
Association of America, ADAA. Accessed June 17, 2019.

https://adaa.org/college-aged-adults-face-less-mental-health-stigma.

12. "Mental Health: A State of Well-being." World Health Organization. August 15, 2014. Accessed June 17, 2019. https://www.who.int/features/factfiles/mental_health/en/.

13. Miller, Matthew J., and Richard M. Lee. "Factorial Invariance of the Asian American Family Conflicts Scale Across Ethnicity, Generational Status, Sex, and Nationality." *Measurement and Evaluation in Counseling and Development* 42, no. 3 (2009): 179-96. doi:10.1177/0748175609344093.

14. Mitchell, Rachel L.C., and Louise H. Phillips. "The Psychological, Neurochemical and Functional Neuroanatomical Mediators of the Effects of Positive and Negative Mood on Executive Functions." *Neuropsychologia* 45, no. 4 (September 7, 2006): 617-29. doi:10.1016/j.neuropsychologia.2006.06.030.

15. "Personality Disorders." National Institute of Mental Health. Accessed July 07, 2019. https://www.nimh.nih.gov/health/statistics/personality-disorders.shtml.

16. "Selective Serotonin Reuptake Inhibitors (SSRIs)." Mayo Clinic. May 17, 2018. Accessed July 12, 2019. https://www.mayoclinic.org/diseases-conditions/depression/in-depth/ssris/art-20044825.

17. "Serotonin." Serotonin | Hormone Health Network. Accessed July 12, 2019. https://www.hormone.org/your-health-and-hormones/glands-and-hormones-a-to-z/hormones/serotonin.

18. Singh, Ajair. "Modern Medicine: Towards Prevention, Cure, Well-being and Longevity." *Mens Sana Monographs* 8, no. 1 (2010): 17. doi:10.4103/0973-1229.58817.

19. "Statistics." National Institute of Mental Health. Accessed July 07, 2019. https://www.nimh.nih.gov/health/statistics/index.shtml.

20. "What Is Depression?" American Psychiatric Association. Accessed July 05, 2019. https://www.psychiatry.org/patients-families/depression/what-is-depression.

Acknowledgements

I want to say thank you from the bottom of my heart to everyone who supported me throughout this writing journey. This is just the beginning, and I am so grateful.

Thank you to Eric Koester and Brian Bies for your incredible patience and thank you for taking on a girl with a love of writing and a fiery passion to make a difference in this crazy world.

Thank you to Maylon Gardner for inspiring me during hard times and reminding me I can make a difference when I actually put my words down on paper.

Thank you to my interviewees who took a step forward and shared their insights and stories— thank you Alex, Ale, Alexis, Eliza, Ena, Jady, Jane Jessica, Justin, Lainey, Nicole, Sigiana, and Sherry. Thank you for sharing your experiences and your knowledge with my future readers and me.

A special thank you to Brittany, Christina, Kelly, and Romina for always helping me spread the news about this topic and my book. This kind of support makes me feel so loved and I am so glad you are a part of my life.

A huge thank you to everyone who actually helped to make this book a reality and allowed me to get published. Thank you for allowing me to pester you incessantly to pre-order. I am beyond grateful for your love and support.

Evelyn Adams	Reyna Colocar	Parker Hudson
Roehl Almeda	CJ Coralejo	Erica Hunter
Melody Apuan	Nicole Corder	Sam Ihns
Lucia Aracely	Caroline Daguinod	Maricar Juachon
Eliza Aretz	Yolanda Dawsey	Jung Kim
Doruthy Arevalo	Aurelia Dayao	Eric Koester
Dylan Ashton	Brandi Dayao	Erin Jane Lapasaran
John Ausejo	Evangeline Dayao	John Edison Lapuz
Alex Bain	Gail Dayao	Devon Leckie
Caitlyn Banania	Geraldine Dayao	Brian S Lee
Lorelie Bautista	Maggie and Benny	Trenton Liberty
Rodel Barcelona	Dayao	Ann Lucas
Kendra Beck	Maria and Fred	Reilly McNamara
Suzanne Dayao	Dayao	Victoria McFarland
Betancourt	Lily Demiranda	Urmilla Medrano
Gabriella Bisecco	Grant Dever	Pierce Mendoza
Romina Bojaxhi	Miezelle Espinoza	John Miller
Margaret Brandon	Craig Fertenbaugh	Selina Minott
Emily Bui	Delaney Fogarty	Merli Morana
Bridgette Burgos	John Adrian Gison	Summer Moskowicz
Jocelyn Burgos	Andrew Glisson	Layne Myhrer
Michael Cassette	Larissa Hamblin	Diane Odra
Grace Changcoco	Kaylah Haseltine	Macaria and Rodrigo
Erin Chatham	Enrique Hernandez	Odra
Jessica Chavarin	Maricar Herrera	Kaitlyn Osborn
Jady Chen	Kyla Hlubek	Let Patalinghug
Lauren Cherry	Emily Hoang	Christina Pfister

Hope Pitman	Kathleen M Stevens	Miranda Valcarcel
Barbara Plaggemars	Meghan Stevens	Ria Viesca
Alessandra Poma	Courtney Stewart	Sherry Warner
Sterling Powell	Rita Story	Holly Washburn
Gabriela Prado	David & Maria	Brittany Watkins
Alyssa Quixley	Stremming	Valesha Watson
Waiming Siu	Eliza Stremming	Lauren Wilkerson
Cheyenne Smith	Erika Stremming	Nicholas Willey
Rebekah Sookdeo	Ena Strikovic	Ashley & Finnley
Militza Soto	Haley Thomas	Winstead
Leslie Stanley	Libby Thompson	Jamie Zimlich
Christina Starling	Makayla Thompson	
Noah Steighner	Susie Upchurch